GROWING WITH THE SEASONS

GROWING WITH THE SEASONS

A Sharing of Insights into the Creative Aspects
of Organic Gardening

Frank and Vicky Giannangelo

SANTA FE

© 2008 by Frank and Vicky Giannangelo. All Rights Reserved.

No part of this book may be reproduced in any form or by any electronic or mechanical means including information storage and retrieval systems without permission in writing from the publisher, except by a reviewer who may quote brief passages in a review.

Sunstone books may be purchased for educational, business, or sales promotional use. For information please write: Special Markets Department, Sunstone Press, P.O. Box 2321, Santa Fe, New Mexico 87504-2321.

Photographs by Vicky Giannangelo
Book design ✺ Vicki Ahl
Body typeface ✺ ITC Clearface ✺ Display typeface ✺ Tempus Sans ITC
Printed on acid free paper

Library of Congress Cataloging-in-Publication Data

Giannangelo, Frank, 1943-
  Growing with the seasons : a sharing of insights into the creative aspects of organic gardening / by Frank and Vicky Giannangelo.
       p. cm.
  ISBN 978-0-86534-626-0 (softcover : alk. paper)
 1. Organic gardening. I. Giannangelo, Vicky, 1942- II. Title.
  SB453.5.G53 2008
  635'.0484--dc22
                                                           2008021250

WWW.SUNSTONEPRESS.COM
SUNSTONE PRESS / POST OFFICE BOX 2321 / SANTA FE, NM 87504-2321 /USA
(505) 988-4418 / ORDERS ONLY (800) 243-5644 / FAX (505) 988-1025

GARDENING, PERSONAL GROWTH
COMMUNITY, AND SUSTAINABLE LIVING

CONTENTS

FOREWORD _____ 13

SPRING _____ 15
    A Springtime Rapprochement / 19
    Hierarchal Atomisms / 23
    Traveling the Tunnel / 25
    Spears of Spring / 27
    Sound Growth / 29
    Rise Again / 31
    Spring Training—Learning Intent / 33
    Moebius Moments / 35
    Planting Partners / 37
    Partial Perspectives / 39
    Precious Harvest / 41
    Baby Steps / 43
    Celebrating Fruits / 45
    A Meaningful Harvest / 47
    Palimpsest Bards / 49
    Efficient Living—Growing Your Worth / 51
    Companion Colonies / 53
    Fractal Gardens / 55
    Spreading Growth / 57
    Garden Hives / 59
    Designing a Context—Stepping Back / 61
    Lost in Anticipation / 63

SUMMER _____ 65
    Consumption of Time / 69
    Continuations / 72
    Listening for the Hunger / 74
    Integral Gardens / 77
    Garden Fluidity / 79
    Growing Genetic Goals / 81
    Direction Meaning / 85
    Building a Conceptual Capacity—A Trellis for Growth / 87
    Vital Vicissitudes—Building a Gateway / 90
    Praxis Relaxes / 93
    Chaordic-Adept Adaptability / 95
    Fluxion to Grade / 97
    Gardening Ourselves / 99
    Life Scales / 101
    The Dancing Hatch / 103
    A Simplex Concern / 105
    Viable Visions / 107
    Recent Returns / 109
    Dependent Independence / 111
    When the Season? / 113

AUTUMN — 115

- Raising a Guest Nest / 119
- Sublimating Vapor / 121
- Gardening the Unus Mundus / 123
- Commonunity / 125
- Residents Resonance / 127
- A Bricolage Mind / 129
- Good Groves / 131
- A Passed Future / 133
- A Preponderance of Chance / 135
- The Garden Obelisk / 137
- Quotidian Dreams / 139
- A Feeling of Proportion / 142
- Laying Layers / 144
- A Stricken World / 147
- Producing Policy—An Open Landscape / 149
- Common Goals—Reproducing a Consistency / 151

WINTER — 153

- Our Share / 157
- Popping as Corn / 160
- A Lingering Glow / 163
- Thanks-Giving—A Natural Service / 165
- Seasonings / 166
- Transition—A Light Behind the Hill / 168
- Proving Grounds / 170
- Vade Macum / 173
- Under the Cover of Events—Down the Road / 175
- Getting in Line / 177
- Filling the Rictus / 179
- A Convincing Self / 181
- Growing Through Perimeters / 183
- Ergodic Remembrance / 185
- Heuristic Naïveté / 187
- A Simple Kernel—Reasons to Grow / 189
- In Roads / 191
- Stretching Out / 193

AFTERWORD — 197
ABOUT THE AUTHORS — 203

A serene reflecting pool

THE SEASONS

"Then sleep the seasons, full of might;
While slowly swells the pod,
And rounds the peach, and in the night
The mushroom bursts the sod.

The winter comes: the frozen rut
Is bound with silver bars;
The white drift heaps against the hut;
And night is pierced with stars."

Coventry Patmore
1823-1896

FOREWORD

We met, fell in love, and married on San Juan Island, Washington. We began gardening together in August of 1986. And, as our gardens grew in size, variety, and complexity, so did we grow in knowledge, technique, and appreciation.

Although we always worked together alone, we were able to share our experiences and insights with others at farmers markets, with garden visitors, the buying public, and by imparting those things learned day by day with other interested, like-minded people who attended our various gardening workshops.

The connection between soul and soil is you and I. Interests may coincide, but it is the spiritual flavors that are tasted in the human communion of growing one's own food, and then sharing it with others. Service attains its highest purpose in sustenance, whether it be physical, mental, or spiritual.

Physical needs are met not only with food, but with shared techniques and methods for its propagation. Enriching the mind entails more than giving it nourishment and vitamins from fresh organic produce; the mind grows and expands by and through concepts that can be proven to be true and beneficial through experience and sharing.

Spiritual yearnings are sated when a combination of the physical and mental energies prove out a harvest of satisfaction effort and appreciation awareness. The garden is a vehicle for a triune creative expression through the coordination of body, mind, and spirit that provides evidence of successful endeavors. It is shared, absorbed, and renewed in its practicality.

In the end, the garden is an anchor that holds us fast to our place in the universe as we confidently work with the materials, energies, and personalities around us to make the world a better place.

Growing with the Seasons is the evolving story of our endeavors to bring about a planned harmony between ourselves, our world, and the people around us. It is our hope that others can use the information and inspiration to create a living chain that someday will secure our planet, and that together we will grow!

SPRING

"The more contemplative gardener, seeing the garden as a whole, the design of it, and its nature as a still place of delight and refreshment, will wait and hope for the moment when it seems to achieve perfection. Awareness of when such moments are most likely helps to make them happen, they will not be entirely accidental but anticipated; everything will be planned to encourage them."

Susan Hill and Rory Stuart

Morning Glory on a trellis

A SPRINGTIME RAPPROCHEMENT

As much as there is a hectic constancy during the spring and summer growing season, during the winter, at 7,300 feet in the clean New Mexico air, there comes a stillness of gardening activity that provides a time for regrouping and reflecting upon ideas, plans, and directions.

Our house, with its continuously bathing wood heat, became a hibernaculum entered into hurriedly and left reluctantly. Snow, melted by the warmth of a late morning sun and then re-frozen in the evening, turned the layers of sand deposited by millennia of sandstone cliff erosion into a shiny brick.

The garden was thought of only when slicing carrots or onions for soups or when cutting up one of the winter squashes. Jars of air-dried spices decorated the lowest shelf of the wire rack in the kitchen. Ristras of dried chiles hung on the wall awaiting their destination in spicy winter meals.

It has been said that failure is a perfect opportunity to look at one's self honestly, and it seems for the gardener that there is always ample opportunity to do this. Those crops that grew in abundance the year before did not do again what we expected of them.

But, our expectations also have certain basic needs, just like plants seeking sun, nutrients, and water. If what we want to happen is to come to fruition, it is necessary to put forth energies in that direction.

In the garden, as in life, there are three basic principles—fact (physical), idea (mental), and relationship (spiritual). There are certain facts that need to be acknowledged: there will be no garden without physical effort, plants deprived of water will wither and die, and neglect will allow weeds to overcome tiny seedlings.

A gardener soon accumulates a list of these physical realities, often noticing that these plant necessities also apply to one's own life. And once acknowledged, we gain a confidence in these universe mechanisms and can work within these energy pathways that exist as natural elements in our lives.

The more we resist finding creative ways of aligning ourselves with these energies, the poorer grows our garden, and our selves. There is a need for an adept adaptability, finding natural creative solutions for the differing environments within which we find ourselves, or our plants.

In our decades of gardening experience, we have had the opportunity to grow in hard clay, sandy, and loamy soils. Each time we have had to use different methods and new solutions to bring about a good harvest. Being inside during much of the winter months allowed time for reflection, a freedom not easily available during the busy spring and summer when we were focused on more immediate needs, like watering.

With the hot New Mexico winds and sun, carefully monitored watering was a must. Often we heard people complaining about the time it took to hand water, so they installed drip irrigation or automatic sprinkling systems. We had always enjoyed watering by hand. Even though we gardened on a fairly large scale, (at times being open seven days a week to the public, servicing restaurants, resorts, and the farmers market), we tried to maintain an individual beauty in the garden. It was only by hand watering that we had the time to view, assess, appreciate each plant, and determine its individual needs as seen within the garden as a whole.

Beauty, or art, is largely a matter of a unification of contrasts; variety is essential to the concept of beauty. We sometimes tend to think that each person is the same even though we know that everyone is unique. Each person or plant is at a different stage of growth and maturity with different needs for that moment which will provide the growth for their fullest potential.

Time spent in a garden allows one to practice focusing and recognizing individual needs. It is an acquired skill that once practiced in the garden can be applied in our lives with equal benefit.

In the garden there grows an abundance of more than just food. There is a connection between the soil (the physical), a conscious plan (the mental), and its execution (the spiritual). The relationship between these elements becomes evident when the most basic of human associations, that of providing food and sharing the bounty of one's labor, reflects the fruits of the spirit (goodness).

What bonds of strength are established at a farmers market when someone buys that bundled bunch of shiny red radishes that will surely bring conversation and comment at an evening meal or a lunch on the patio with a cool summer salad?

What neighbor turns away a gift of food, energizing in its freshness, bringing health and a feeling of well being? A gardener does not grow only for self, or profit, although it is an honest earning, a satisfaction hard to come by these days.

Everyone desires to be in harmony with the physical, mental, and spiritual aspects of the universe. The rapid march of invention and progress has, within recent history, veered and broken ties that gave us identification with our place and compatibility with cosmic progress. These lost connections have increased the difficulty to proceed toward goals of the future, those greater than our present selves.

We had put the garden "to bed" for the winter. Seed catalogues accumulated in our post office box in town, often crammed in tightly because we do not go often to collect the mail. Each year seed companies sent out ever more sophisticated advertising with glossier paper, brighter photos, newer and better hybrids. A few retain a studied, nostalgic feel. The chasm between their seeds and our garden was wide.

For us, gardening is "growth," but for seed companies, as Marshall McLuhan has noted, "All advertising advertises advertising." Even so, one cannot help but see the catalogs and think about the next growing season: what would be done the same way, what would be changed, and with what new ideas?

So much of a garden is based on a logical analysis of what is needed to provide the basics. Plants do not grow by themselves and neither do we. Our nutrients are creativity, progress, and that inner knowing of what is the right direction.

Master Fwap, a Tantric Buddhist teacher, speaks of our having a "second attention," one that is outside the structures of logical analysis. This second attention depends upon careful timing and rapid, accurate adaptataions within the mind. For us, planting and harvesting took on a realization of that "right moment" followed by frenetic activity.

It was as if a propitious moment had snuck up on us, and we turned around to find it within our grasp. Then, with a trusting belief, we acted, using it to its greatest expression and advantage.

Spirit is receptive, material is reflective. In spring, when the moon is right and the weather says, "take a chance," an archaic call stirs within us. We re-establish that harmonious relationship with the universe in the garden—a reflection of the realities of Truth, Beauty, and Goodness—and we grow.

HIERARCHAL ATOMISMS

One can tell approximately how close spring planting is by many factors. One is how much snow and ice has receded or disappeared from the north side of the house. It is always the last to go, building accumulations from each snow, melting slightly and refreezing with each cold period, creating a mini-glacier that holds its iciness until spring when it finally disappears, not returning until next winter.

Another sure sign to be counted on was seen one day as we drove to Gallup. Next to the road there were two prairie dogs warming their alert bellies, standing tall next to their dens just in case a quick escape was needed.

In the greenhouse, seeds had germinated, grown, and needed to be transplanted into larger containers. On the rock ledge against the stucco wall, a pink hyacinth given to us by our neighbor had opened, sharing with us its vibrant color and sweet fragrance.

Our world is not one of singularities, but of systems. The snowmelt behind the house involves the sun and shadows, freezing temperatures, and moisture from oceans that accumulates and falls. Prairie dogs feel the warming earth creeping down into their dens like a thermal alarm clock, urging them upward.

Our friend who gave us the hyacinth knew that it would be only after the sun began returning to the lengthening sky that we would be able to pause while transplanting to see and smell what had been promised.

The physics of complex systems, (*Homeokinetics*), designates these systems as "atomisms," systems repeated in structure and character that can withstand "forces of intersection without permanently deforming." The disappearing snow, the appearance of prairie dogs, and the blooming of the hyacinth are all atomisms—systems of actions bringing eventual change.

Gardeners utilize atomisms to produce their crops—combining water, soil, fertilizer, and other elements—all systems within themselves. We then employ these systems as individuals, using them to tell the story of a collective. We direct this story using a common language: seeds, heating mats, greenhouses, and potting soil.

We all understand, or at least learn as we participate, where this language will lead us. It becomes a catalytic process that evokes action, and with seed catalogues in hand, we pursue those potential images.

When evoking these events we become hierarchs, "stewards of sacred rites." The process of planting seeds is a memory function that gathers generations of seasons, and propels the gardener onward using an ancient common language of rejuvenation.

Like Brownian particles, constantly changing motion and direction, we move to the tune of invisible forces, unerringly responding to the melting snow, the emerging prairie dogs, and the opening hyacinth—the call is unmistakable, the direction unalterable, and the mandate undeniable—we must grow!

TRAVELING THE TUNNEL

It had been a year of patient waiting for that one brief moment when the sun would rise and shoot across the eastern mesa, its morning rays suddenly bright through the clerestory window, lighting a long narrow rectangle of fused glass, an equinox marker graciously made by a friend and local artisan especially for the occasion.

The intricate patterns of glowing colored fused glass evoked the feeling of some archaic hieroglyphic, meaningful, but unreadable. It seemed only moments had passed when the sun's movement left the narrow rectangle.

Our friends, the glassmakers, were there to witness the event and shared a green chile casserole, some sweet rolls and coffee. After the meal, lingering on the deck, warmed by the risen sun and a second cup of coffee, we invited them to come again to witness the sun's rays on the second glass rectangle that would capture light at sunrise on winter solstice.

Photos of that moment would give reason and evidence for the wait from the time we first climbed a ladder and outlined the dimensions of where glass should be. We have suggested to others this idea of using the outside environment to personalize the inside of one's home, much as one's garden provides an outside association with nature's seasons.

These longer days have slowed the disappearing woodpile, leaving just enough on the front porch to meet our needs. The large goldfish in the pool outside were rising to the surface and mouthing, "feed me." More seed trays had been planted and daily went back and forth from outside on the deck to back inside the house before sunset, the nights still in the low twenties.

Although most gardens contain a variety of plants there is usually one special plant that is the gardener's favorite. Ours were probably chile plants, with Habanero, Jalapeno, Cayenne, and Poblano heading the list. We fell into this naturally because they grew well in this area, and we used them in almost everything we ate. They also had a wonderful practicality—canned as condiments or jellies they became welcomed gifts for others. Strung in colorful ristras, they provided that southwest ambiance to one's home, whether outside the front door as a greeting, or hanging in the kitchen as a seasoning-at-hand.

The vernal equinox in spring is like the mouth of a tunnel that we enter and travel through, exiting out the autumnal equinox at the other end. Timothy Leary coined the phrase, "reality tunnel" as part of a concept that everyone interprets this same world differently. This term "reality tunnel," can also apply to groups of people united by beliefs and actions, hence have we entered with others into a "gardener's reality tunnel."

We all enter it at the same time at spring equinox, and will exit it together at the autumn equinox. Along the way we all will plant, nurture, and harvest. Our gardens represent the same world differently, expressing our desire to be in a certain harmony with the universe.

The *Talmud* teaches that, "We do not see things as they are; we see things as we are." When our lives and our gardens promote beauty and goodness, then we will grow.

SPEARS OF SPRING

One spring, after we finished sifting the compost near our old garden, we decided to go in and look around, not expecting to find anything other than weeds, since we had allowed it to become fallow and return to its previous natural state. To our surprise, around the edges there were tulips. We dug them up and heeled them into the sifted compost. In the middle of the garden, we found daffodils and a few grape hyacinths, which we dug up and put in the compost for the ride home.

Taking one more walk around, we noticed heads of asparagus poking up through the dirt. One spear had arrived too early in the season and had frozen. Upon closer inspection, we found more coming up. By prodding with the shovel, we were able to find main root balls that were six or seven years old.

Asparagus reaches its prime after six to eight years and can remain a good producing plant for about fifteen years. It is a member of the lily family. Its name is from the Greek, meaning "sprout" or "shoot." Cultivation around the Mediterranean had been going on for thousands of years, but it was first domesticated by the Macedonians around two-hundred B.C. Asparagus was used not only as a food, but also as a medicine. It contains no fat or cholesterol, is low in sodium, and is a nutrient-dense food high in folic acid, calcium, potassium, vitamins B1, B6, A, C, and E. It has diuretic properties and is a good source of fiber, and rutin. The amino acid *asparagines* derives its name from asparagus. Chinese herbalists use asparagus roots, which contain steroidal glycosides, to help reduce inflammation.

We took the plants home and dug a deep trench, added compost, gypsum, and bone meal to help reduce transplant shock, and watered it well. Then we planted the crowns about six inches deep and five inches apart, covered them with soil, watered them again, and applied three inches of mulch.

The Dutch and English brought asparagus to this continent in the 1700s. These original plantings were unimproved, non-hybrids called "Washington Varieties," named after Waltham and Mary Martha Washington. Today, hybrids used commercially and in home gardens are divided between those for the northern climates, (the Jersey varieties available through most garden catalogues) and a variety called UC-157 used in the southwest, California, and Mexico.

Asparagus is a herbaceous perennial plant with stout stems that mature into a many-branched feathery foliage. It prefers a humus-rich soil and it is best to use the results of a soil test to provide a complete and balanced mix of nitrogen, phosphorus, and potassium (NPK). Throughout the season, the young whips, and spears, can be eaten raw, grilled, or boiled, although we enjoyed them steamed or sautéed, and served with butter or with a dip. Because it only took a few minutes to cook asparagus, the Roman Emperor Augustus coined the phrase, "velocius quam aspargi coquantur," or "faster than you can cook asparagus."

One of the more unusual features of asparagus is the smell of one's urine shortly after eating it. There are disputes as to the exact compound, but it is formed as a derivative during digestion when some of the constituents that naturally occur in asparagus are metabolized and excreted in the urine.

We always looked forward to harvesting them throughout the season, which usually lasted from early spring until late summer, at which time we allowed the last spears to grow into ferns—the factories that supplied energy to the crown and storage roots that nurtured the next year's crop.

These early spears of spring reified our winter garden images, as did the vegetable transplants that we carefully spaced in the GreenzBox™ (a self-contained growing box covered with shade cloth).

This turn of the season awakened us suddenly from a mental garden to an edible epiphany. Our own winter ferning had resupplied us with the energy to bring about once again, the renewing affirmation of the garden and the eternal fact that we were growing.

Aspargus spear

SOUND GROWTH

Our moisture for the winter finally came in early spring with a couple of snowstorms that blew through, leaving everyone with various depths of accumulation, depending upon where they lived. The deepest was about two to three feet along the Zuni Mountains to the north of us. The winds swept up the side of the range and then dropped the moisture at the base.

Water is of concern to all people in all places, but it is even more valued in naturally dry areas. With the global-warming-shifting-weather patterns, this area has experienced long periods of cyclic drought. Drought has been cited as a cause in the disappearance of large groups of ancient peoples in the American southwest, who built sizable communities and then suddenly abandoned them.

The history of water on earth extends back over four billion years to the accretion of water from comets and hydrous asteroids. Seventy percent of the earth's surface is water, eighty percent of fruits and vegetables is water, and H_2O is the most recognized chemical code.

Hydration of our bodies is as important as the hydration of our plants. On an average, two and a half liters of water escape our bodies each day, sixty-five percent in urine and feces, twenty percent through our skin, and fifteen percent through our lungs. We remembered from school the diagrams and arrows showing the water cycle of evaporation, precipitation, and run off.

The 2003 Nobel Prize for Chemistry was awarded for the discovery of the aquaporin, a tiny passageway into a cell that allows only one molecule of water at a time to enter, even though the cell is surrounded by water. When a cell hydrates, it triggers an anabolic phase of building and repair that helps keep us healthy. This transfer of water dissolves nutrients, removes waste and toxins, and activates cellular energy. For every molecule of protein in the human body, there are ten thousand water molecules, more water than is needed for each cell, or that can be dealt with at one time.

We might also remember diagrams showing how "structural matching" is necessary for two molecular objects to exchange information and activate a needed response. This molecular interaction, sometimes also called the *Key/Keyhole Model*, happens according to current theory, as a random collision on a trial and error basis.

J. Benveniste suggests that instead, electromagnetic signals traveling through the body's water are what really activate specific functions. These signals are low frequency electromagnetic waves, much like those used by submarines for communication, since megahertz frequencies do not penetrate water.

Every atom of every molecule emits a specific frequency. Specific frequencies of water molecules can be detected at distances of billions of light years by radio telescopes. Water can carry and amplify communication between corresponding molecules to bring about desired chemical productions.

The topic of memory in water has been explored for decades; memory not as consciousness, but as leftover "imprints," influences in the form of electrical information or electromagnetic waves that can affect the flow of information through the water's molecular structure.

Masaru Emoto takes this even further in his book, *The Message from Water,* claiming that water reflects the composite energies being sent to it by restructuring the molecules into crystalline structures resulting in either "positive" or "negative" formations. Water not only has the ability to reflect the environment but it also can be affected by the quality of our intentions and thoughts.

The quality of life thus depends upon the signals exchanged between molecules. This co-resonance is much like a transmitter and a radio; we can hear the message when we are tuned into the frequency.

Our lives exist within a water cycle that flows in and out of our bodies, our plants, and our earth, and if we listen and co-resonate, we will grow.

RISE AGAIN

Easter, the annual Christian festival in commemoration of the resurrection of Jesus, (from the Latin, *Resurrection(as)*, meaning *to rise again*) is observed on the first Sunday after the first full moon after the vernal, or spring, equinox.

Winter had again provided rest, and a quiet period of contemplation. We were ready once more to "rise again," knowing the battles to be fought, with new ideas, knowledge, and enthusiasm, to select, plant, and nurture our seedlings.

The garden's first call to spring arrived after we had just finished a general cleaning in the garden, and had attached the last batten on a new greenhouse, now almost ready for use. The warmth of the morning sun foretold of temperatures that would continue to rise until there would be no morning frosts.

Even so, the previous year a killing frost had occurred after even the most cautious had set out their tender plants—squash, peppers, and tomatoes—only to find them blackened in the morning. But, we would "rise again" trying to get an advance on the short summer growing season by putting out plants when we thought we "knew" it was safe.

The bright green spires of garlic we had planted in the fall "rose again" through their blanket of thick brown mulch, their bulbs formed from the previous year's crop of cloves. We ate the smaller ones, and replanted the largest cloves. They had been planted in early September, because we realized that at our altitude they needed more time in the fall to establish their roots, which are the foundation for the best and largest garlic cloves.

Another aspect of the garden that soon changed was daylight savings time, altering our waking and gardening habits. Mornings were darker but the hours available for working later increased. We adjusted to the springtime functions of starting seedlings in the greenhouse, transplanting them into four-inch pots, and to the needs of the beds in the garden that called for nutrients, organic matter, seeds, and the transplants. As the season quickly approached, we rose once again to pursue the highest blessing of all human activities, working with the soil.

We who garden know the resurrection formula of the universe: Truth—we plant a radish, and get a radish. Beauty—the sun, water, and air give us the fruits of our labor. And, Goodness—which comes when we share our bounty; dinners with good friends, the farmer's market, or a bouquet of garden flowers given to a neighbor as a "thinking of you" remembrance.

We "rise again" to grow our lives, planting into our souls those seeds that will sprout within the systems of the universe, growing what we value: those truths, that beauty, and the goodness, preceding us and coming after us, as we grow.

SPRING TRAINING
Learning Intent

Although there were snow patches left here and there outside, in the greenhouse there were patches of green. The trays of seeds and seedlings, the beginning of another spring planting, were spaced and rotated from the heating mat that encouraged germination, to the holding area for maximum light and growth. No matter how many times we had done this, it always seemed as if there was some small step in the process that was missed, not forgotten, but needed to be remembered, a nagging vagueness that made one review what they had learned in order to find the omitted detail.

Soon our bodies had to reconnect with contorted stances and the strange body positions needed for spring gardening preparations. The first few activities needed to be slow and easy, warming up the body lubricants to free them from their frozen winter positions. Activities stretched muscles in unfamiliar directions and when continued too long, surprised us in the morning like an unfamiliar alarm clock going off. There are not many other activities we do that produce exactly those movements, those yoga-like stances with names like, "leaning with hoe" or, "seeding bent over."

Reorganization in our mind takes some effort. Where did we leave this, what happened to that, and why didn't we have any of what we needed? Corralling resources entailed combining the partial, the nonexistent, and the needed. We found it useful to make a list of the needed, checking off the nonexistent, and relocating the partial bags of blood meal, bone meal, and any other nutrients or additives that had been in the basement staying dry for the winter.

Tools had somehow migrated, each to their own place, hiding, waiting, and resting. As each was found, attention was given to its condition. What was needed to refurbish it to make it workable? Sometimes it was just a matter of cleaning and oiling like with the Mantis tiller. Other tools needed a bit more help. Our warren hoe had a crack in the handle for years but we had continued to keep it together with duct tape. Warren hoes, for some reason, were hard to find in this part of the country, so we added another layer of tape and kept it functioning.

The inner urge to grow a garden, at times can seem vague, and make us wonder why we would want to go to all that trouble?

One reason was that we had been lulled into a winter-supermarket-convenience-complacency that hid the memory of fresh lettuce and kale salads, with moisture filled shredded beets and new baby carrots providing splashing colors and tastes, and of course, fresh picked radishes adding a crisp "snap." Other reasons for wondering why grow a garden resurfaced when we remembered all the time needed to go from seed to table, the applied resources, and the dedication of continual care.

We often think of the grocery store as an extension of our food choice chain. We forget about what Marshal McLuhan calls the "amputation" that results when we view or make use of something that extends our bodies and minds, but in the end deprives us of hard earned skills and associations: tilling, composting, germinating, transplanting, and the joy of harvest.

Some results from our self-amputation are the pollution of our genetic pools by mega-gro corporations, the pollution of our environment, our natural resources, and our health. We tend to be so immersed in our extensions as an integral "necessity" of our life we forget how the car amputates the pleasure of walking, so even the thought of eliminating or modifying an extension is quickly passed over.

As gardeners, we know the benefits of good pruning, weeding, thinning, and selecting. If we apply these to our extensions, we will grow.

MOEBIUS MOMENTS

In the spring, it was always tempting to try to get a jump on the growing season. However, after some rational thought, past experience prevailed and delayed the heartbreak of planting too early and being hit with the late frosts common to New Mexico high desert areas.

We moved up the hillside into the new hogan we built where flat areas were hard to find and the deep bedrock of sandstone protruded, giving little chance for cultivation of the soil. Beginning again in a new area with new conditions and a slightly warmer microclimate, we limited the gardens to the most utilitarian for our diets. Culinary herbs, carrots, beets, lettuce, cucumbers, different varieties of chard and kale, green onions, summer squash, butternut squash to store for the winter, and salad greens like arugula and cilantro had been planted in raised rock beds filled with compost.

We trellised the butternut squash and cucumbers on hog wire fencing to prevent damage to leaves and save space. Behind them, we planted scarlet runner beans and blue morning glories that would climb up the back of a coyote fence that separated the garden from the parking area.

One Saturday in May, we had a workshop on sustainable organic gardening. Among the participants were eight Native Americans from the Pueblo of Acoma. There were two adults, and six students from high school who were members of the Acoma Boys and Girls Club.

The topic of traditional growing methods came up and they mentioned that they were attending the workshop because drought and cultural changes had effected their growing conditions so much that a new approach was needed, one that incorporated both the knowledge of their elders and modern gardening methods.

In 1855 August Ferdinand Möbius, a German mathematician (1790-1868), discovered what has come to be known as the Möbius Strip, created by taking a paper strip and giving it a half-twist and merging the ends together to form a single strip.

One of the almost magical properties it possesses is that when cut down the middle along a line parallel to its edge, instead of getting two strips, it becomes one long strip with two half-twists. More cuttings produce exotic figures with names like paradromic rings and trefoil knot. This feature was demonstrated by M.C. Escher in a lithograph showing a line of ants crawling on the surface of a Möbius Strip, some on the outside of the strip and some on the inside, but all on the same path.

The seasons of the year also promote a Möbius Strip behavior in that, while on the same path of pursuit, we are sometimes inside and sometimes outside the path. At this time of year, we approach the twist that takes us from the inside to the outside. Seedlings yearn to get out of their containers and into the ground, an urge shared with the gardener.

The bend of winter leads us into the bend of spring. As we each move along the path of our strip, we share knowledge gathered along the way, and together we grow.

Baby Butternut Squash

PLANTING PARTNERS

All but one of the twenty-four rosemary clones in their seed tray had rooted. On the heat mat beside them, thyme, blue flax, basil, red rhubarb, and sage had begun to germinate, poking their first leaves up out of the soil. Once up to size, we would transplant them into four-inch pots, label them, and wait for the local plant sale, and the farmers market.

We were fortunate to have been helpmates in gardening. Over the years, we had learned the most economical division of labor, allowing us to not only get things done easier, but faster. It is not that one of us could not do what the other did, but experience had allocated certain chores to each.

The word partner comes from Latin, the combination of, *a piece* and *co-heir* (part + parcener). Thus, as partners, we were both inheritors of the garden's fruits. While we were partners as husband and wife, we had other partners in the gardening process—a community extending out in a twenty-mile, and growing, radius.

These community partnerships were evidenced at local gatherings where information or goods were exchanged. Part of the local lingo was the phrase, "going to town." What it meant was that a person was going either to Grants, Gallup, or Albuquerque, rather than just down the road to the local trading post or post office. There was always a willingness of someone to get that one needed item, saving another the one-hundred mile round trip.

Gates, cattle guards, and fences that keep out livestock were used as "drop off points." The mail, items bought, or things borrowed and returned, were tied in plastic bags and could often be seen fluttering on a gate.

We sent our gardening newsletter out to subscribers all over the world, and we never knew what response it would bring. Through the years, we had received emails from those for whom some bit of information was just what they needed, or others who could identify with something we did in the garden, an event in the community, or just life in general.

We often felt like the newsletter was being posted on some gate or fence, returning or receiving some small piece of information or goods too far away for someone to go and get at the time. As planting partners in the planning and development of our planet's future, the subscribers and we became *co-heirs* to its destiny.

We looked forward to spring and the first tips of daffodils urging up through the soil. One of the great things about daffodils is that they multiply and soon produce small groups, or colonies. Given enough time, they can grow into fields.

Like colonizing daffodils, we find ourselves in a profound propinquity, pointing to a many-paged future that will tell the story of how we grew.

PARTIAL PERSPECTIVES

Looking out our bedroom window, we could see only a portion of the coyote fence we put up on the west side of the garden, meant to help ease the strong spring west winds that started about ten in the morning and blew until sunset.

Originally, coyote fencing was sticks and pieces of broken juniper put together by Navajo or Mexican sheepherders to form corrals for the night protection of sheep from coyotes.

Now old juniper fence posts are used, those that have rotted off at ground level, once being eight feet, now reduced to six or less. Old fence posts were also used for other purposes. One friend used it to hide her propane tank down the hill, both from her view, and any neighbors across the field who may have been able to see its robin's egg blue color sitting amidst the sandstone hues. Another friend enclosed her small back yard, providing a containment and definition for the grassy area and formal gardens existing amid sandstone spires and multicolored cliffs.

Adverse conditions promote symbiotic relationships; most of the trees around us grew together, intertwined. The piñon pine and the juniper mingle, providing a component necessary to weather this environment. Hence, the juniper never grows straight; it weaves and works its way around the piñon.

Most juniper fence posts (the wood that will last the longest) have at least two, if not three, bends, curves, and twists to them. The trick in using them for coyote fencing was to be able to adapt these curves to the post on either side, creating a fence of continuity, with not too many wide gaps. We often had to turn a post upside down to make it fit.

A "partial perspective" is in many ways like building a coyote fence. Each next part must "fit," as well as possible, to the bends and curves.

With the first leaf erupting plants (radishes, lettuce, spinach, and onions), we had a partial perspective of the coming year's garden. Whereas the perspective of the coyote fence from the bedroom window was rendered partial by trees, a view of the garden's final fruition is obscured by time. No year in the growing season is ever the same, and the gardener must twist and turn to each new situation: the heat, the wind, the lack of rain, late or early frosts, and all the other events that appear during a growing season.

With the coyote fence, the adjustments were made visually. With a garden, adjustments were made with, and by, experience, knowledge, and information. Each required a step-by-step process to achieve the goal.

Over the years of growing, we had accumulated many facts, things we knew worked. We had also read about more things than we had been able to put into practice, and we held these as knowledge or ideas to be used if the need should arise. We constantly ran into information (in magazines or books, on television gardening shows, pamphlets, internet sites) that provided a link, or relationship, between all of the facts that we had accumulated.

Just as we gathered the posts for the garden fence, we provided the soil with nutrients, tilled it, and put on a layer of mulch. Seeds had been planted and just as we adapted the twists and turns of the posts for the coyote fence, we would twist and turn ourselves to grow a garden that would "fit" into the new season as we grew.

Catmint

PRECIOUS HARVEST

Living in a small rural community usually means everyone knows each other. Whenever we met friends and neighbors, the first question usually asked was, "How is your garden doing?" Some asked if anything was ready yet. We had been harvesting a lot of rhubarb and asparagus, but as far as the other crops, they were just getting started.

We were still having frosts and had not put out the vulnerable plants— peppers, tomatoes, eggplants, melons, cucumbers, and squashes. Later in the season when we saw these folks at the farm, or at the farmer's market, they were able to see what was ready and enjoy the harvest. We can imagine this scene being familiar in neighborhoods and small towns everywhere.

Being a gardener allows for early harvests that can't be readily shared. One of the first harvests for us was prepared soil. Looking over all the beds that had been given nutrients, tilled, and covered with an even layer of mulch gave a certain satisfaction, a knowing that our first steps in the garden journey had been in the right direction.

Our next bountiful harvest came after planting the early spring seeds that were nestled into little "valleys" made by pulling back the mulch. Peas, radishes, onions, beets, carrots, spinach, and lettuce needed consistent moisture to germinate and the constant spring winds that stripped the moisture from the top of the soil just above the seeds made daily watering a must.

No matter how many times we had seen them, there was always a thrill when those first specks of green poked through the soil. As they got larger, they showed that spring "vividness of green" that is never matched. It might just have been the contrast of new green to the majority of brown, or the sun still climbing and shining at an advantageous slant. Maybe not having seen much green throughout the long winter days produced this brightness.

Standing and watering allowed for the inspection of each row, each plant, and the time to look around and to be able to watch the cloud shadows that ran across the fields below. There was time to smile at the swallows twisting and turning above, and to pull out the weeds that we missed last time.

We liked to think of it as "weed and water" time (they slipped out easily when the ground was wet). It is one of the gardener's "productive pleasures," a precious harvest. While watering, the mind is allowed time to wander, assessing immediate and future needs, refinements, and additions.

Once more, we went down that familiar but ever changing garden path. These beginnings provided the fruits of harvest that gave inspiration, re-determination, appreciation, and satisfaction—a "harvest of confidence."

This process places us in the growth groove of the universe, flowing with the elements towards fruition and a later harvest, one that can be more readily shared with friends and neighbors as we grow.

BABY STEPS

It's warm, it's cold. Spring promotes those stutter steps that lead to planting cautiously. It's a start and stop process, temperatures surging into the seventies or eighties during the day, and nights dropping into the twenties. Gardeners always, it seems, are looking for that opening of opportunity to get a jump on the growing season, to say, "My peas are up," or "I set out my cabbages and they haven't frozen."

We enter into a growing season not by leaps and bounds, but in increments, surging ahead when we feel we can and then holding back when we know we can't. This is good. It allows us to opt into a process that is best suited for our tasks.

Each year we took out the tiller and prepared to work the soil, and although we had done this many years, each was in some way new and different, and other year's procedures felt a bit askew.

One year, to combat loss of moisture, we introduced perlite. Perlite is volcanic rock that has been heated until it explodes (much like popcorn) producing small pellets that have indentations around the surface that allow water to collect in them to await a searching root. We added it not so much because of the heat, but because of the early spring winds that wicked the moisture from below.

Water consumption should be on the mind of every gardener, even if their water supply is more than adequate. Early season water loss prevents transplants and seeds from achieving maximum growth. Feeder roots, if they dry out, do not continue to accept nutrients and need to be re-hydrated to revive their feeding mode. So, rather than a steady growth pattern, they are much like our beginning garden forays, start and stop. Whereas we can benefit by this choppy start, the plants do not. The best plant growth comes when a constant and consistent environment of maximum growth potential is applied: available nutrients and water.

Although we had some of the potentials for maximum production, new elements always appeared that made us take baby steps. It sometimes took us awhile to be appreciative of this slow beginning; we generally wanted to jump in with both feet going at maximum speed. Adding the perlite made our tilling rhythms different.

The first bed went somewhat slow, since we needed to adjust to mixing the soil like we wanted it to be. This was done step-by-step until we were able to get up to full speed, having learned what to do while taking small steps. Those baby steps allowed us to choose the best process, rather than trying to run from the start with what we thought we knew was best.

Adaptation is always a part of each growing season, just as adaptation is a part of our life's growth. Using baby steps productively assimilates new elements and factors, in our gardens and in our lives. Seasonal abilities and knowledge are guided into present proficiencies.

No matter how fast we want that seed to become a radish, it needs to take its own baby steps to fruition, just as we take our own steps to fruition so that we can grow.

White Daffodil

CELEBRATING FRUITS

One night we received a phone call from an old friend in Idaho. Eventually the talk turned to gardens. He was excited to tell us that he had eaten the first squash from his garden for dinner that evening, and we were able to tell him that we had just eaten the first salad from our garden.

First fruits seemed to hold a greater sentiment for us than when the summer garden hits full production and salads and greens became daily fare. Tastes buried in our memory were suddenly revived by that first Poblano pepper we picked that was growing in a container sitting on the deck. These fruits from the garden helped us put the world in scale. No longer was our food tied so tightly to sources outside of our control.

Our first salad that year was raised in compost, sifted from a couple of aged piles, leftovers from the growth of the other years' gardens, and the good deep green color of our seedlings showed that there was plenty of nitrogen to insure steady, healthy growth.

The earth's atmosphere is composed of about eighty percent nitrogen, more than we could use in a lifetime. But in order for nitrogen atoms, which are all tightly bonded, to be of use for our plants, they must be separated and joined with hydrogen atoms. We rejoice when rainstorms with lightning break this bond and attach nitrogen to hydrogen atoms, which results in "fertilized rain."

In 1909, Fritz Haber, a Jewish German chemist, discovered how to take nitrogen from the air and produce fixed nitrogen by a process of heat and pressure produced by electricity.

Before that discovery, available nitrogen was produced either by animal manure, lightning, or by leguminous plants like peas or alfalfa, which take nitrogen atoms from the air and "fix" them into useful molecules by soil bacteria living in their roots. Without available nitrogen, life cannot assemble amino acids, proteins, or nucleic acids. An average human body contains almost a kilo of nitrogen.

Synthetic nitrogen, ammonium nitrate, became popular after WW II when it was used as a chemical fertilizer for farming instead of explosives for war. Once produced commercially, it became the darling of mega-farms, who no longer had to use animal manures to provide nitrogen for their crops. The crop that garnered the greatest application was corn, using more than half of all synthetic nitrogen produced. Corn produced everyday items we that we don't usually think of: linoleum, fiberglass, color in processed foods, joint compounds, and, of course, high fructose corn syrup.

More chemical nitrogen was applied to crops than they could use, and the excess evaporated into the air acidifying the rain, contributing to global warming. It also seeped into the ground waters, streams, and rivers, ending up in the Gulf of Mexico where it stimulated algae growth to the point of smothering fish and creating a "hypoxic zone" as large as New Jersey, and still growing.

For now, we have celebrations with old friends, new friends, organic foods, and a hope for new directions in which we will grow.

A MEANINGFUL HARVEST

One evening we walked through the garden with friends, and when we reached the asparagus bed, the question arose: when once planted, do you wait to harvest for three years to let the roots become fully established, or just begin harvesting the first year, regardless of root age?

With us was a gardener and early settler who had lived in our area for eighty some years, so we asked his opinion, knowing that he had kept an asparagus bed growing for a long time. His reply was simple: he looked up at us grinning and said, "If it comes up, eat it."

While this appeared to be a simple answer on the surface, we knew there was more to it from listening to many of his stories about the hardships and struggles of those early days when there were just dirt roads, no phones, and no electricity. There was no help in case of an emergency, only those who lived nearby, and preparing for winter was a very serious endeavor.

Whether true, needed, or right, there was a certain luxury in planting asparagus that first year and then standing by watching as the fresh green shoots emerged, grew, and ferned out into their "providing energy for their roots" stage, when they were no longer edible.

A local grocery store also provided this luxury for many people on the planet. The threat of winter and its lack of food had given way to strolls down aisles stacked with out-of-season fruits and greens kept fresh by automated misters, and a constant culling and tossing away of vegetables that had no need to meet a crisis standard.

In different times, we would have been grateful for one of those wilted dark edged heads of lettuce, or a slightly limp carrot. Gone, for most of us, were the days of winter-driven internal sensations that would have led us to plan, plant, and preserve.

While we walked down the produce aisle to check the prices of veggies (so we could price our own goods within a competitive range at the farmers market) each display evoked a certain feeling, a physical sensation of association. The radishes and carrots gave that feeling of the patience needed to thin and separate the weakest from the strongest and healthiest. With eyes focused onto a small area, one had to decide which would go and which would stay. There was always that twinge of regret at having to pull one, not having been diligent enough at planting time to space the seeds properly.

After so many seasons, the internal sensation began to take on meaning for the value of the activity itself, gardening. Meaning is something that experience adds to value.

Surviving winter was an experience that provided early settlers with a different meaning for their food, other than the value of sustenance. This meaning was internal, as was the value, both of which had to be felt to be known.

We didn't have a garden just to grow food. We had it for the experiences that promoted values and expanded meanings. And, when the season was over, we could share the new meanings, and grow.

The first spring Iris

PALIMPSEST BARDS

One spring we were most fortunate to have the weather turn warm, the wind and scattered snow of only a few days before, passed on to the east. There were twenty-two of us sitting out in the sun, wiggling the plastic patio chairs back and forth to anchor the legs firmly into the sand.

Our friend, and guest speaker/poet/gardener, kicked off the second half of our sustainable organic gardening workshop by discussing the value of a garden as inspiration, not only for writing, but also for personal insights. A couple of poems were read by him (not his, he was a modest fellow) and then followed by two of his own gardening related poems, (he was not that modest).

Our group consisted of a woman from the Women's Intercultural Center, ten young people from the Youth Conservation Corps, two sisters from Catholic Charities, and others, young and old, locals and out-of-towners.

We had gone through all the handouts, the basics, the hard-wired facts about fertilizers, soil building, intercropping, compost, seedlings, and mulch, along with the questions and answers that would always arise. We had just been to the gardens, checked on the composting worms, walked the labyrinth, viewed the greenhouses, and ran the tiller, with a few of the braver ones doing some "hands-on."

After eating our sack lunches and getting to know one another better as we shared this picnic meal, it was time to get some inspiration, some ideas and thoughts that were more guidingly abstract.

After a period of time each went to reflect; some, sitting by a pool of water with its gentle re-circulated splashing, the friendly cats rubbing and asking for attention, while others went out in the garden or to the labyrinth. A few went over to the chicken coop taking their cues from the continuous clucking, and others walked out into the fields to feel and see the vista of cow pastures and sandstone cliffs, with the Zuni mountains as a backdrop in the distance. Tim and his poetry were to help each compose their reflections of the workshop experience

We re-assembled in our chairs, rattling papers with furtive glances. Once one person had read what they had written, others wanted to read, albeit with some self-conscious hesitancy. There were rhymes, haiku, free verse, and our own personal doggerel. There were insights, flashes of felt moments, and humorous lines that set us all to laughing, young and old, and one memorable poem about our Mantis tiller that garnered applause.

A palimpsest (from the Latin, *palimpsest*, meaning *to be rubbed or scraped*) is a manuscript of parchment upon which the writing has been erased or partially scraped off, and a new text is simply written over the old. Such is a garden. Each year we scraped away what we, as bards, had written the year before with our seeds and plants.

We revised last year's manuscript by scraping away the old, and that which had accumulated over winter, to create a new, clear surface upon which we would write the next year's message to the world. Some things were retained; the perennials, the herbs, and the returning flowers escaped our clearing as we held onto them and worked around them. We increased our vocabulary with new varieties and added verve with adjectives of color.

At times, as we wrote over last year's verse, words or phrases may have appeared from beneath, speaking gently of the past and our commingling with it. Each year we wrote with new voices on that same piece of manuscript that we valued, as the parchment around us was torn into smaller and smaller pieces by agribusiness and development. How valuable that piece became when we had written our beliefs, our hopes, and our desires upon it. How easily it was read when others saw the spring green, plainly speaking from the dark, wet ground.

Could anyone mistake our words when seeing the results of plants bursting forth in paragraphs of colors? As we shared our manuscript, no one had doubts as to the salads of our sentences.

The stories we write are old. A parchment is available to all. Each person's writing provides another chapter of illumination, progressing toward the final book of cooperation and collaboration, speaking out for the benefit of all. And, in the end, it will say we have grown.

EFFICIENT LIVING
Growing Your Worth

For us, "efficient living" was working in the present in such a manner as to enhance the values of the future by the conservation of resources. One way was to conserve water, since water tables and aquifers were lower than they had been in years past.

Long-range weather forecasts, becoming more accurate in forewarning possibilities of drought, demanded steps toward actions that would help deal with the problem in a practical manner.

"Old timers," who had lived more than eighty years in our area, told us it had indeed been a very dry year. Others, who didn't have that accumulation of experience, yet had seen more years go by than we, agreed. We had always been big believers in mulching as a means of water conservation, but sometimes, good mulch was hard to come by.

Our previous mulch source had been from helping a friend clean out an indoor goat stall/shed, which would accumulate eight to twelve inches of hoof-packed alfalfa, goat poop, and urine. After loading and taking it home, we broke it apart and crumpled it by hand into a consistent-sized mulch, a process that often took two or three days.

At one organic gardening workshop, we met someone who owned a shredder, and he mentioned if we ever wanted to borrow it, call. We called. We had worked with different types of shredders over the years. One was a commercial sized monster that was almost scary to approach. It was unbelievably fast, sucking in brush, limbs or whatever and spitting out chips at the other end.

Other shredders we had used proved troublesome and frequently clogged (materials too wet, too fibrous, this, that, or the other), so when we picked up the borrowed shredder it was with some thoughts of shredders past as we loaded it into the truck. Three of us lifted it easily into the bed and strapped it down for the ride home. It was an 8HP Craftsman.

It was small, easily portable, but powerful. It didn't use hammers so it didn't clog once. We put through fresh bales of alfalfa, old alfalfa, the goat barn cleanings, and some old, dried garden vegetation. It literally threw the evenly chopped pieces out the back with such a force we had to stop and build a three-sided containment area using cement blocks, with a sheet of plywood for a roof.

With other shredders, as the shredded material built up on the ground, we had to stop and pitchfork it into a pile next to the shredder. This machine blew it out with such force that it "piled" itself against the back of the container. Not once did we have to stop to relocate the shredded material and it only took a few hours instead of days. We can say without reservation that this was the best shredder we had ever encountered.

The previous week had produced very high winds that blew our freshly tilled beds dry often taking the topsoil away. We lost both soil and nutrients, but by the "luck of the draw," we acquired a machine that gave us what we needed: a deep efficient mulch, consistent sized, easily procured and produced. And, once it was watered, it formed a crust that prevented the wind from blowing it away.

We had a tool and hope for overcoming one of the elements of adversity that was not only indigenous to our area, but that was expected to increase in intensity in the future. This extra deep mulch was efficient, practical, and would enhance values of the future; conserving water, a greater productivity using fewer resources, and less impact from our lives in areas that we affected.

By so doing, we enhanced our worth to the world's progress toward good. We would produce more, and use less. By efficient living, we could grow.

Sweet peas on a trellis

COMPANION COLONIES

Not all our food comes from our gardens. One afternoon we drove into Ramah, a small town about twelve miles from where we lived. We met a truck, along with others who would unload what we had ordered through the Tucson Cooperative Warehouse.

The semi-truck pulled onto a side street, one of two in the town, and those who bought through the co-op unloaded the boxes into their trucks and Jeeps and took them to a member's house to be sorted and divided. It was fun being with friends you didn't get to see very often, doing something you all believed in, like the food co-op. And, it didn't matter how much you bought, one person ordered one package of organic coffee, while someone else's order filled two pages.

A colony is a group of the same kind, living together in close association. We were the same kind because we wanted organically grown foods. We enjoyed participating in the co-op because it was a convenience for us and we didn't have to drive fifty or a hundred miles to enjoy the range of choices that we had to choose from in the monthly catalog. We ordered in bulk so the prices were lower than they were in the organic retail stores. One of our favorite products was organic Mediterranean olives that came all the way from Turkey.

You often hear the terms "organic this and that" without thinking of those doing the gardening, farming, or packaging. We lived in a close association with olive farmers because even though the company was not local, we could easily get them. They grew organic olives; we grew organic vegetables. So really, it all came back to food, and in our isolated rural area, eating was high on the list of things to do.

Even though our garden was not producing food at that moment, elsewhere there were others of like-mindedness providing what we wanted. Exchanging foods makes us all companions (from the Latin, *companion*, meaning *messmate; com-with; pan-bread*).

Sometimes being a colony is no more than people being in the same area catalog shopping. By doing this, we supported not only each other, but also those with similar ideas halfway across a world made more compressed by a jar of olives.

In spring, our greenhouse got fuller by the day with seedlings and transplants. The time was rapidly approaching when, in a way, we would become the coop, taking fresh organic foods to people who were not able to grow their own, shrinking the world, and making them our messmates.

At dinner, with salad from New Mexico, olives from Turkey, and other foods from around the world, we grew, and become an international colony.

FRACTAL GARDENS

One day as we neared the Jeep in the parking lot, we could see a message left on the windshield; it was from the UPS woman parked across the lot by the post office. She had a package, glad to be able to deliver it to us right there rather than drive down a muddy road she had already been stuck in once before.

We were not too surprised when we read on the label that it was from *Seeds of Change*. We had found their large selection of organic seed to be mature, of good quality, with a high rate of germination. It had only been a day or two since our seed trays had been filled with potting soil and the heating mat brought up from the basement into the greenhouse.

The lengthening days had melted all the snow except those spots on the extreme northeast side of trees and buildings. Out in the garden, the garlic planted last fall had started to grow, reaching skyward, taking in the sun's energy. Several clumps of Johnny Jump Ups were blooming, showing their bright colors against the backdrop of melting snow.

While looking for the heating mat, we had glanced at our Mantis tiller ready and waiting to be filled with gas and have its tines dropped into the earth to help prepare the soil for spring planting. We felt suddenly that we were again at that yearly threshold of creative potential. Rituals like this allowed us to escape the limiting boundaries of our everyday lives, and returned us to a place of discovery and creativity at the system's edge.

Once within the garden, we ceased to be a mechanic, a salesperson, a businessperson, or a teacher. Those titles and jobs fell away, along with much of the human activity that fostered dissent and unrest. Instead, we were able to clothe ourselves with an underlying attitude and direction that promoted emancipation and conviviality.

In these arrested times we find our global view of man's place in the cosmos, and carry it with us back into society, allowing it to aid in the restructuring of that society. According to Victor Turner, "Ritual is a principal means by which society grows and moves into the future."

Benoit Mandelbrot, one of the founding fathers of fractal theory, found that chaos can become ordered; "When the values fed into an equation are themselves the results of that equation's previous calculation, an infinitely variegated, yet ordered and self-similar pattern emerges."

Thus, we "feed" each year's garden, iterating the actions and knowledge from those years previous, our ritual providing a gateway, allowing us to expand our information and reveal creativity. These become tools for change.

Our beliefs are then utilized in "morphic fields of pattern perception." When we return to the social structures, where our individual actions have a "collective aspect that is synergistic in impact," we promote change and "feed" what Sandra Braman called "horizontal evolution," a worldwide human unfolding through concurrent interactions.

Our world stands on the threshold of status quo, the "crowd mind," influencing the outcome of social and economic tendencies. In desiring these tendencies to change, we can take heart from an encouraging fact drawn from chaos theory called the "butterfly effect" (when a butterfly flaps its wings in South America, ripples are felt in Kansas).

What we feed the social equation repeatedly will eventually create a self-similar pattern, actualizing a frontier, a new threshold from which we can step, and entering into communion as equal individuals, we can grow.

SPREADING GROWTH

Try as we may, we can't stop growing plants and making gardens. We had attempted to reduce the number of plants considerably, but they continued to appear as if by magic, popping up in rock gardens and containers on the deck.

It's as if spring mornings had switched on an auto-gardening relay to our brains, and suddenly we found ourselves with shovels, rakes, and trowels in our hands, digging, sifting compost, fertilizing, and transplanting seedlings from seed trays that seemed to just fill up with soil and were planted. At times it seemed like we had performed invisible activities and the results were stumbled upon during our daily routines. Gardening had been a life routine for us for decades, and the necessities entailed in the process were second nature to us, ones that appeared with increasing daylight and then disappeared with its decline.

In 1976, Richard Dawkins, a British zoologist, introduced a concept that referred to a "Unit of Cultural Information." This unit of information was designated by the term "meme" when addressing the transfer of an idea, concept, or practice, verbally or by demonstration, from one mind to another. For the most part, the method of transferring a meme is by demonstration. Transferring the benefits of gardening by demonstration does not mean that one must give lessons. What we see often unconsciously transfers to our beliefs.

Just as our genes turn on and off impulses that control chemicals in the body, so do memes turn on and off ideas and concepts in our minds. In our bodies, once these chemicals are created, they join in the changing of the body's needs to aid in the perpetuation of physical life. The meme, once transferred, also takes on a life of its own in the mind of the one in whom it was transplanted.

Like the process of gardening, it is akin to popping out a plug from a seed tray and transplanting it into a garden setting, where it will become part of something larger, giving influence to the whole.

One of the results of this meme transfer is the desire to plant gardens, grow in containers on the deck, and take care of houseplants. Frank's mother had a Crown of Thorns plant that was over fifty years old, and whenever she watered it, he could feel in her care a joy of association. It wound, spiraled, and twisted, with new green tips showing all over, entertaining to the eye and satisfying to the soul.

In 1995, Iaccomo Rizzolati of the University of Parma discovered what have become known as "mirror neurons." The group of mirror neurons that fire in our brain are the same group as those that are firing in the brain of the one we are observing, and therefore allow us to directly understand the meaning of actions and emotions of others through an internal neural replication of those events.

We do not need objective reasoning to understand, because through the mirror neurons we are able to have a direct simulation linking us to that other person. When someone sees us caring for our plants, they gain and grow from our joy and appreciation by association and viewing.

The purpose of osmosis is to diffuse from one part to another and produce a commonality or equalization. By a caring demonstration of our plants and gardens, we establish a mental osmosis within others. Once this nurturing concept has been transplanted, those who see it have this information in the garden of their minds to use in beautifying and enhancing the garden of the world. Thus the seeds from a single caring demonstration can be spread to others who will understand and feel this intention to grow.

GARDEN HIVES

The rains that eluded our area in past summers were constant company late this spring. Some New Mexico cities had problems with flooding at lower elevations.

Our rural areas experienced problems with the one and two lane dirt roads that allowed people access to highway 53. Some roads became too muddy to drive on, some washed out completely leaving deep, v-shaped trenches. Others were stripped of their gravel as water cascaded down from the mesa tops in a torrent, washing across the road leaving humps of sand gathering on the exposed sandstone and bedrock. The rain produced an abundance of vegetables for the local farmers market, and fields filled with wildflowers that carpeted the valley floors with intermingled patches of purple, red, and white.

This newfound beauty held observers in a wondering state, not having this scene in recent memory. The grama grass, growing knee high in waves of purple, prompted old timers to say, "The snow in winter will be as high as the grama grass," and how many inches of rain had fallen in each area pervaded every conversation.

In the spring, when we started seeds in trays using a heating mat, seedlings emerged from the soil within just a few days. The garden at its maturity supersedes the collective of seeds that were in the trays. Each plant emerged as part of a whole-garden pattern, and no matter how well imagined, the pattern would not be visible until completed.

This collective growing process is a common natural phenomenon, an instinctive grouping mechanism in life cycles, much like a hive of honeybees. Individual bees make up a hive integrated for the all bees in the community—the workers, the drones, and the queen—the identity of the beehive carried through its collective memory.

According to Kevin Kelly, one speck of a honeybee brain has a memory of six days, whereas the hive as a whole has a memory of three months, twice as long as the average bee life. This collective thought called the "hive mind," is the continuation medium.

When a colony gets too crowded or becomes weak, it will swarm. Honeybee swarms are an instinctive part of the life cycle of a bee colony, providing a mechanism for the colony to reproduce itself and grow. Each garden can be thought of as a vegetable hive.

The garden's continuation medium is the genetic memory in each annual, biennial, or perennial variety as it merges into the pattern of the whole garden.

The marvel of the "hive mind" is that, no one is in control, and yet an invisible hand governs. The same invisible hand that governs the hive is the hand that tells the gardener when to plant and when to harvest. Just as there is nothing in the bee hive that can't be found in the bee, there is nothing in the seed that can't be found in the garden as well as the gardener. Each is part of a vivisystem that is greater than the individual.

One day enough garden hives will reach the point where we will need to swarm; an invisible hand will move us toward a higher and greater purpose, and once there, as our new seeds are sown, we will grow.

Rock steps in a perennial garden

DESIGNING A CONTEXT
Stepping Back

We found it amazing that labyrinths were mentioned in almost every magazine we opened, from *AARP* (a senior citizens publication) to *New Mexico Magazine*. Turning on the television one evening and flipping through a few channels brought us to the sight of people in a church where the pews were pushed back to reveal an intricate, mosaic labyrinth on the floor where they were walking slowly and solemnly around the pattern in spiritual association.

A labyrinth is different from a maze. It has one path to the middle and from its center the same path back leads back out. In a maze, dead ends can be around any corner, forcing you to backtrack and search for another way in or out. To walk a labyrinth is an internal journey, a "period of practice," in which we focus on and reinforce our deepest intents.

It wasn't long ago that travel to exotic places all over the planet expanded our perspectives, concepts and views of our place in the universe. Serial satellites showed us on high definition television screens not only the sight of once faraway places, but intricate and intimate details of foreign lives, mingling in our homes with other data devices that allow us to speak with them if we wish. The Hubble telescope transmits to us pictures from distances that were they received instantaneously, may not even exist.

Despite returning snows, our first seeds had been sown, the heating mat turned on, and the warmth inside the greenhouse had germinated cotyledons that were up to catch the light.

When we noticed some had not sprouted, there was always the temptation to start "digging around to see what was wrong." Usually the only thing wrong was our impatience. Each seed has its own appearance program and can't be forced to germinate before its time.

Some aspects of gardening lend themselves to a policy of "*laissez faire*." Recognizing these uninfluenciable intangibles allows us to pause in our forward rush to go from "seed to feed" and realize that the desire to "do something" is effective only after we have, from experience, found those actions that are in keeping with the step by step procedures already well established in nature. Today, more than ever, it seems to our advantage to take the time and be aware of that natural development.

Marshal McLuhan noted that causality became open to scrutiny when electricity made things happen instantaneously, ending for us an appearance of sequence.

Entering the garden is much like entering a labyrinth. With that first step, we head toward a "center." Step-by-step we know there are no dead ends that will make us doubt our choice of direction.

The working harmonies of the garden also bring us strength, perspective, insight, courage, knowledge and wisdom. We enter into a sacred space that reminds us of our true purpose of existence, a life filled with meaning, value, and spiritual growth. We are renewed when we enter into that actual physical reality which is no longer just a thought within.

The goal is to walk our everyday lives within a "living labyrinth," reflecting ideal reactions, relationships, and interactions. It is up to us as to how and what we will grow.

LOST IN ANTICIPATION

It seems popular these days to use the term "living in the moment." This advice is often given to someone who is concerned about an aspect of the future and feels powerless to do anything about it. The immediacy of our shrinking world covers us with situations in which we had no hand; what is happening today is not a part of our yesterday. This can make "living in the moment" an alienated affair, like being made to watch a TV show chosen by someone else, and not being able to change the channel.

Probably our favorite thing to do for relaxation was to take our dogs for a long walk. The area surrounding us was once inhabited by various native peoples who left sherds and detritus from their day-by-day living. Each piece found was interesting, a connection with a people like us who also wondered about the future—a future with more immediate effects. Their "living in the moment" was planning how to survive the coming winter by gathering enough food from a less than hundred-mile radius.

It was easy to spot anomalies on our sandy ground, pieces of flint, chert, and obsidian appeared as small reminders of a previous inhabitation, and every now and then, there was an arrowhead, a mano, or some other tool they used in their everyday lives. Keeping an eye on the ground often caused us to walk right into tree branches. We became lost in the anticipation of what was next, not knowing where we were at the moment.

In the garden, the first planting of beets and carrots peeked through the soil. As spring developed, our walks got shorter, usually leading us back to the garden to look for crop anomalies—weeds. When people commented on the lack of weeds in our gardens, and what a problem it was for them, we tried to let them know that, for us, weeding was an "action-meditation". We laughed and remarked that being "lost in a weeding moment" often brought new ideas, insights, or solutions to problems.

Anticipation and gardening go hand-in-hand. There are three aspects of anticipation (from the Latin, *anticipat,* meaning *taken before*) that every gardener must have.

The first is an ability to foresee when the weather will be good for planting, when the moon be right for good seed germination, and how many growing days there might be.

A second factor of anticipation is expectation. What we can expect from our garden is fresh organic food, culinary herbs, flowers, good exercise, and the sharing of evening dinners with good friends.

Thirdly, we must anticipate the actions that tilling, planting, weeding, and harvesting will bring: that sense of satisfaction, and a connection with others, reaching out to bridge the distances that separate us. Gardens become the ambassadors of our anticipation for the future, in which we will grow.

SUMMER

*"We may have to learn again the mystery
of the garden: how it's external characteristics
model the heart itself, and how the soul is a
garden enclosed, our own perpetual paradise
where we can be refreshed and restored."*

Thomas Moore

Iris, catmint, a kitty, and thyme

CONSUMPTION OF TIME

Sunny summer days not only took away the memory of past snowy days, but melted the few lingering patches of physical evidence into the ground, leaving its presence to be evidenced by growth of abundant greenery. These same snows had earlier relegated any gardening activity to a planning and review stage.

As we designed a new abode, we perforce, curtailed our gardening scale, still growing for farmers market, but in anticipation of a new, full time effort of construction, we halved the growing capacity of our large vegetable gardens.

After construction was completed and we were ensconced in the new hogan, smaller surrounding garden areas were created and planted. Not satisfied with the few herbs and plants, we built a raised bed garden that more than satisfied our hunger for fresh organic greens. Even though we had access to local, fresh, greens at the farmers market, the personal factor of self-reliance proved to be a lacking quality.

Trial and error provide some of the greatest lessons in life, especially when the trial ends in error. It is then, in the spirit of conservation, that we are able to use our imagination, talents, and creativity to rescue and re-define our original intent.

Traditionally, where we live, summers are set in two stages: strong winds with hot days (eighty degrees) and cool evenings (frosts) during late spring, with an influx of bothersome gnats in June that drive some locals to take extended vacations for the entire month. Then there is the welcome arrival of the monsoon season during July and August, cooling the latter part of the day and delivering ion rich rain to the gardens below.

New Mexico was in a drought situation when we received the long anticipated rains and snows. We had hoped for such a return of moisture and planned ahead by having a backhoe dig out a large ravine for a pond area at the bottom of a hill. The dirt that was taken out formed a dam to retain the water that would be channeled into it. We didn't have long to wait and we weren't disappointed, except for the fact that we had not yet installed a rubber pond liner.

Much of the hill behind us is exposed Dakota sandstone, a cretaceous sedimentary layer deposited when the sea covered this area around one hundred million years ago. When rain falls upon it, there

Squash growing up the coyote fence

is little absorption. Instead, it acts like a roof, collecting the water and sending it down the hill in rivulets. We knew this and had dug a gutter-like trench for water diversion, guiding it around the hogan and down into the pond.

We were excited and proud as the first big rain of the season came down. Inside, we watched, running from window to window as the water ran down the trenches and diverted into the pond, collecting as planned. It didn't take long to fill it three-quarters full.

It wasn't but a day or so later when the next monsoon blew in. This time there was so much rain that it overflowed the trench we thought would be able to handle it all. We watched in apprehension as the pond quickly filled and went over the top of the dam cutting a "v" which quickly widened with the push of incoming water until suddenly, the whole dam gave way and the pond became a streambed.

We were at the bottom of a north slope, which received little of the declining sun during the winter. The pond was farther away from the hill and received a lot of sun on its steep, south facing slope. We decided to use this side of the ex-pond and reconfigure it into a gardening area.

By terracing the slope, we would be able to take advantage of its depth for wind protection, and by using sandstone rock for the retaining walls we would have a radiant heat source for cool spring evenings, preventing frost damage and thereby extending the growing season. We could also cut into the bank and build a cold frame-greenhouse, using the surrounding earth for insulation. So, instead of a large fishpond, our hole had become a cynosure of adaptation.

Wenda Gu, a Chinese artist, noted that human knowledge in general is nothing but an artistic interpretation. Just as food provides energy for our day's endeavors, time allows for the digestion of events, by which transformation we will grow.

CONTINUATIONS

Lately our household watchword has been, "eat more salad," not because of the obvious health benefits of growing our own organic food, but because there was so much coming out of the garden, even though it was the smallest garden we ever had.

Scattered around the southeast side of our hogan were ornamental beds with zucchini, culinary herbs, and rhubarb, tucked in amongst perennial flowers. In large containers on the deck were Poblano peppers, several varieties of tomatoes, and cucumbers.

Sugar snap peas, butternut squash, and morning glories climbed up the posts on the outside edge of the covered east-facing porch in front of our door.

A raised bed running north/south, protected from the hot afternoon sun by an area of small trees to the west, was covered with shade cloth. We opened the shade cloth on the east side every morning for direct sun. The shade cloth left on top provided needed shade during the heat of the day until the sun fell behind the trees.

The biggest change (from the Latin, *cambire,* meaning *to exchange, trading one thing for another*) that we noticed from using shade cloth was the size and tenderness of the salad greens. Benefiting from the coolness, they gave us giant, tender leaves that just melted in our mouths. The idea of using shade cloth in our previous gardens had always been in the back of our minds, and we had talked about it, but the size of the gardens presented obstacles that we were unwilling to deal with at the time.

Smithsonian Magazine once ran an article on the production of a new form of recyclable plastic made from corn called polylactic acid (PLA). This resin was used for forming containers and other packaging of consumer goods. It was known as a "principle compostable," meaning it would break down into harmless natural compounds. At present, conventional plastics take up twenty-five percent of the volume of materials sent to dumps. They also use an estimated two-hundred-thousand gallons of oil a day for their production.

Within the article, the carping ran from the fact that PLA would not break down in a home composting operation, to complaints that PLA would interfere with conventional composting because it needed more oxygen than present systems have.

The production of PLA uses sixty-five percent less energy and generates sixty-eight percent fewer greenhouse gasses than the production of the more common polyethylene terephthalate (PET) found in the ubiquitous soda pop or water bottle. One would think that these pluses alone would cause immediate cheers and changes. Growing food commercially by agri-businesses represents a field of concerns: genetic diversity, organics, packaging, transportation, and individual responsibility.

But, as with most change, there is a reluctance to exchange one thing for another, no matter what the benefits might be. We believe most people desire beneficial changes for the world, but often feel impotent by the smallness of their individual actions.

The first corn plastic was made about twenty years ago at a cost of two-hundred dollars a pound. Later Patrick and Sally Gruber, both chemists, created a prototype PLA product on their kitchen stove at a cost of less than a dollar a pound.

Sometimes the anxiety of change is that it will never arrive. This feeling can cause people to give up whatever they are doing toward beneficial change. It is persistence of an idea that keeps it alive until conditions are right, and then its implementation becomes a success.

Many paths headed in the same direction will eventually meet, and from these well-established beginnings, the world will grow.

A cucumber blossom

LISTENING FOR THE HUNGER

We have seen so many variations on the bumper sticker that reads "Think Locally, Act Globally," "Think Globally, Act Locally," "Think Universally, Act Globally/Locally," and "Think Locally, Act Universally."

Now, right away, we know the universe is going to get a bit harder to handle, a little more than we want to bite off, much less chew. Even attempting a global act at this time feels intimidating. But perhaps we may be able to be successful on a local front, nothing too pretentious, just "Thinking Locally, Acting Locally."

It is interesting how once knowledge of the whole increases, belief in the self decreases. Ages ago, knowing how to grow food or other crops was not a secret, or an area within which only a few could

Bugs n' flowers

function. As plant-world knowledge increased, it became more of a specialized field, one occupied by those with a "green thumb."

Fresh market availability and the ever-expanding mega-farms relegated those who had no time or purpose for gardening to the "brown thumb" category.

It is common to overhear conversations about how the CIA is watching each of us from high definition satellite cameras, the Illuminati are in control of the world's finances and begin wars to increase their fortunes, or that conspiracies by organized religion are preventing us from knowing some Truth that, were it revealed, would bring confusion and despair to millions.

Another recent conjecture that has garnered attention is the dispute over whether evolution, the result of a fortuitous mixturing of space chemicals of which we are the result, is true, or if life began, as some Creationists claim, on a four-thousand year old Earth.

Without a framework within which to place, use, and accept the ever mounting supply of facts, figures, ideas, and inventions, confronting global events can leave one unprepared and unknowing about what to do next, somewhat like walking into the greenhouse and suddenly discovering an overwhelming total infestation of aphids.

Ilya Prigogine discovered how physical systems, designated by him as "dissipative systems," are able to convert disorder into order when subjected to "high-energy input."

As any gardener knows, elements exist independently until certain specific conditions drive them to organize into a coherent whole. Together these specific conditions help bring about congregation and organization for a common purpose.

Slime molds are composed of thousands of amoebas that live individual lives, but come together when hungry. Their combined hunger vibration is the signal of need that when reaching a critical point, congregates and organizes them into a single unit which will then move to a desired feeding location and there sprout stalks and a body from which spores are ejected and new amoebas are born to renew the process.

Our gardens produce foods for the mind, body, and soul. At present, we feed mostly bodies. But, hunger within the mind and soul will someday increase in vibrational need, reaching that critical point where humankind will congregate, organize, and move to a new level and a new place from which we will satisfy more than the body's hunger with a world-wide willingness to grow.

A perennial garden inside the straw bale wall

INTEGRAL GARDENS

Usually during summers, we receive monsoon rains in the mid-afternoon, but for the last few years, they have been erratic. We had noted this trend, and did not plant our usual large vegetable garden for the farmers market. Instead, we planted one small bed with a few vegetables for ourselves and interspersed chard and kale among the formal perennial gardens inside the strawbale wall that surrounded our house. In the greenhouse, we planted tomatoes, cucumbers, and peppers.

The thick, strawbale wall around the house and gardens created an *ecotone* (a place where two ecological worlds intersect, or overlap). Living in an *ecotone* demands adaptation to both zones.

We are fortunate in that when the land surrounding us was "chained" around 1950 to make room for more pasture, they left nine big piñon pines (which we pruned) standing close together allowing their tops to form a large canopy of shade. This canopy diffused the intense sun at our altitude of 7,300 feet, creating perfect shaded conditions for gardening in this climate. Part of the fun of gardening is finding creative ways to adapt to the conditions around you.

Outside the wall were grasses, wildflowers, shrubs, and weeds, growing and dying, contributing to the varied green and brownish colors in the landscape. The spring rains that year kept things relatively green, an event that usually didn't happen until mid-summer.

Our gardens were comparatively small, but impressive when one entered through the gate because they were so contrastive with the world outside the wall. The sound of a water fountain bubbling in the reflection pool combined with the sight of a lush formal garden often became a memorable experience.

Gardens can also provide examples of sequential evolutionary stages that are analogous to the cultural stages described in the "integral philosophy" of Clare Graves. She was one of the first to note how stages of individual human development are "a recapitulation of the stages of human history." Plants also have comparable stages.

We had observed radishes going from seed, to maturity, to becoming seed bearers; beginning as "tribal" shoots, all looking alike with their Mickey Mouse-eared leaves, and then individualizing into their own unique shapes and colors. According to Graves, plants, humans, and all life, began in "archaic consciousness," developing into "tribal consciousness," and then defined individuality by growing into a "warrior consciousness."

"Traditional consciousness" is achieved by a symbiotic relationship with the whole—much like companion planting promotes the well-being of each individual plant in relationship to the garden as a whole.

Science created the "modernist consciousness" through worldwide communication capabilities. The next level will be a "postmodern consciousness," which calls for a more "worldcentric recognition" of the planet and the relationships of people living on it.

Gardeners experience one of the desired traits of a "postmodern consciousness" when they exhibit a "sensitivity to the fragility of the environment." We can notice a plant's slightest droop, or see a color that is not quite vibrant enough, and respond with some curative action.

The food we grow and then share with others, is an across-the-board continuing paradigm that transcends cultures, politics, and philosophies. It is the continuing thread holding together the fabric sewn from a living history of being.

We had guests for dinner one night. We sat in the garden patio under a canopy of trees surrounded by a protective wall where we ate, visited, and nourished our bodies with fresh kale salad, our minds with laughter, and we elevated our spirits when we drank deep from the panacea elixir of good cheer. And thus well nourished, we grew.

GARDEN FLUIDITY

Our tomato plant in the green house was in full production and produced lots of sweet, medium size round tomatoes, and when they were picked a bit early, ripened to a deep red as they sat on the sunny kitchen windowsill.

Some years back we had received a packet of tomato seeds from a seed company asking us to plant them as experimental seed and report back on how they did. They were simply called, "Number Nine." We continued to save seeds from that first planting years ago still using them for the plants that grew in our greenhouse.

Initially we planted them outside in the main garden, where they struggled when the temperature fell below fifty-five degrees at night, but the ones planted in the greenhouse attached to our house thrived.

Gardeners harness many energies and forces. They take a seed and begin to circle around it, from inspection and selection to preparing the ground, providing light, nutrients, and water. We were always concerned when the carrot seeds, planted good and early, had not broken ground in two or three weeks. We began prodding, looking for green, gently lifting off soil with the tip of a knife. Soon seedlings did appear and grew quickly, but we still kept a watchful eye on the process, especially since we so carefully spaced them when we planted them.

As they grew larger, they needed us less, especially after we had thinned them, allowing space for each one to reach full size. When we harvested them, it was hard to imagine that big Chantenay carrot was once such a tiny seed.

When we adjust the pH of our soil, we are creating a medium for electromagnetic transfer. Crops always seem to get greener and grow faster after a couple of good soaking rains full of ionized water.

When a new garden is created, it seems to take about three years to get it adjusted to all the levels of energies we come into contact with. Previously learned methods are used, adapted, adjusted, and healthy plant growth validates our choices, the plants become mature, and the end results give us next year's techniques and a better working knowledge of our garden's world.

Anaxagoras, 2,500 years ago, put forth the idea of reality being formed out of vortices. The transfer of an idea into a reality is much like the planting of a seed, and from that point on, the reality of the seed in our physical presence grows like a spiral, ever widening its influence on our time and efforts.

Once seeds are planted, we circle on the vertex of the spiral, the highest point, the greatest distance from the seed. As the season progresses, we travel further away from our planted seeds into a sea of vortices, a vegetative ether through which we maneuver toward a goal of fruition.

Once initiated, these spirals of influence continue widening out and away from our personal vicinity. Each tomato is a seed of influence, when once placed into motion by being shared, becomes a portion of the larger whole created with each season's garden.

Just as our gardens are made up of different plants—each providing its influence on the garden as an entity—so does each person give their direction and tone to the energizing world reality that we, together, are creating—eventually producing a fruit that will benefit the world as a whole—providing humanity with the nutrition and the certainty that we can grow.

Claret Cup cactus blossom

GROWING GENETIC GOALS

The world's first geneticists were gardeners. Although not knowing the cause of a plant's behavior, observation recorded the result and the seeds were passed on from generation to generation as "family heirlooms." We still use observation and collection of specific seeds to produce crops that we know will "run true."

The dependability of a plant to continue to produce desired results is a hidden factor. We cannot, without special instruments, see the guiding instructions that are within each cell of every plant we grow.

So, we must then look to known characteristics that have come about as a result of interactions with the environment. For example, most northern plants have shorter growing times than their southerly cousins.

We find these effects of nature to be observable modifiers, which switch on and off certain expressions within the plant's DNA. Studies have shown that an organism responds to the environment by switching on previously "silent" genes (infrons) to aid in creating a response to a threat within that environment: heat, wind, soil conditions, etc.

And, once these genes have finished with their task of adaptation and progression, they are "switched off" and other genes then take over to promote the next stage of necessary development.

This process in the plant world can be seen in a few pockets of vegetation in Appalachia and on the Ozark Plateau where there exist plant species such as Neuiusia alabamensis (Alabama Snowwreath) discovered in 1857, yet remarkably similar to those in the region twenty-four million years ago.

Recently, the theory of genetic Darwinism of random change through mutation has been challenged by Rhawn Joseph in his new book, "*Astrobiology: The Origins of Life and the Death of Darwinism.*" He states that, "Contrary to Darwinism . . . the evidence now clearly indicates, that the evolution of life has been genetically predetermined and precoded . . ." The Human Genome Project seems to agree, noting that new genes are produced only under "precise regulatory control."

Over 100 years ago a Swedish scientist, Svante Arrhenius, introduced the idea of "panspermia," a thesis that life on earth was seeded from beyond. This concept has been approached from various perspectives as varied as Fred Hoyle and Chandra Wickrawasinghe, claiming living cells were delivered to this planet by comets, to Francis Crick, co-discoverer of the double helix structure of the DNA molecule, who came to the conclusion that life was so miraculous that it was from a process of "directed panspermia."

However delivered to earth, once initiated into action, evolution has unfolded in accordance with specific DNA-based instruction which had been inherited from the first life to appear on this planet. So has plant life evolved from its early ancestors to the present day vegetables we now grow and mutually recognize. We are also able to recognize the needs of those plants—the NPK (nitrogen, phosphorus, and potassium) of the DNA.

Today, we are losing species rather than acquiring newly attuned plants that have evolved in response to the trends of climatic growing conditions. Two important plants, soybeans and corn, are being "dead-ended" by genetic botanists resulting in seeds that commit biologic suicide.

Mapping the human genome has prompted a search—a returning to nature—for plants that may be of benefit: aspirin from willow bark, Taxol from the yew tree, etc. The earth itself has become a repository for possible cures. Soil collected from Easter Island has produced a compound to prevent kidney rejection, and a modified version of a bacterium found in garden soil is being tested as an anticancer agent.

After a reign of synthetics, scientists are rethinking the natural world, and the latest studies show that within our DNA, prior to the disease which makes them necessary, exist the instructions to produce lymphocytes (antibodies—killer cells that attack foreign bodies) for any disease.

All of these results point to what Rhawn Joseph calls the theory of "Evolutionary Metamorphosis." We are growing as we change—as individuals, as a society, as a culture, and as a world within a universe. We have arrived at a biologic limen, having been sent by an infinite patience, to this moment in time and space.

The interaction between two objects is a relationship, but three or more objects eventuate a system. Will we choose to create a system that will produce seed good only for one crop and then be of no use, or will we finally choose a realization that within a cosmic system the individual members are not connected with each other except, in relation to the whole, and through the individuality of the whole?

When will we listen to the apriori instructions whispering within each cell telling us how to grow?

Penstemon palmari (wild pink snapdragon)

The main vegetable garden

DIRECTIONAL MEANING

On occasion, we hear the saying that, "the shortest distance between two points is a straight line." This is true, yet not an applicable guideline for gardening. For us at least, we have never been able to just plant a seed and reap a harvest without circumventing insects, drought, weeds, and all of the other exigencies that seek to detour us from our goal.

Locally, there was already talk of grasshoppers this year, that there would be no rains until July sometime, and although not detrimental to crops, the dreaded appearance of very small gnats in June that whine near our ears and bite unseen. They are repellent proof and make outside endeavors so miserable that some plan their vacations away from the area for that single reason, and do not return until after the Fourth of July, the traditional day marking the first rains and the end of "gnat season."

For those who don't flee, remedies and preventatives are freely given: baby oil (they drown in it but the blowing sand will cover and stick to you), this cream and that lotion, and, of course, the advice to just cover up from head to toe, including fine mesh nets draped over one's favorite summer hat. For the most part, none claimed great success.

With us, for some reason, they enjoy the tops of our ears. We can hear when they are near their landing strip and often wave a quick hand or two back and forth by our ears to prevent them from landing. These gnats are an annual event and just as the spring winds are expected and dealt with, each person copes in his or her own way.

A familiar act becomes an institution when given structure and goals that will, in the end, be inspiring and comforting. The garden has provided structure from the earliest attempts to ward off winter starvation by growing an excess of immediate need. Inspiration comes when our personal efforts show progress by using tools developed in pursuit of the goal.

It was comforting to have homegrown organic carrots, onions, beets, cabbage, and garlic, stored for the winter's use; red and green peppers strung and hung to dry; a good supply of catnip and culinary herbs dried and put in jars. For the gardener, "comfort food" takes on a new meaning. It is comforting at the end of the growing season to be able to say, "We did it," or, "We're done." It allows for a proficiency of expression that is hard to find these days. Another outcome is that we have become better at dealing with the day-to-day vicissitudes of life.

Our ability for self-maintenance is increased when we can better direct the paths, the changes in our lives. Knowing the correct turn puts us on a direct line between two points that, although not straight, is nonetheless the shortest distance and sure of directional meaning.

In 1923, Alexander G. Gurvich discovered biophotons, a light emission that is "an expression of the functional state of the living organism." This light is thought to be constantly absorbed and released by DNA molecules stored in our cells, forming a communication network with all of life's processes.

Our gardens are biophotonic expressions within which we deal with the mutating realities we commonly confront. But, with a well-lit path and goal, we can grow.

BUILDING A CONCEPTUAL CAPACITY
A Trellis for Growth

Just how much location can play as a part in our thinking, appeared suddenly when once remembering a garden from the past. The main components of a garden are often narrowed down to nutrients, seeds, and water, to a point that the tributaries of other ideas are not used.

When we left Arizona and bought our property in New Mexico, we discovered there were some old telephone poles lying on the ground. We largely ignored them at the time, having other goals to accomplish, like building a house, cleaning a space in the old horse corral for a future garden, finding a job, and all the other matters that arise when relocating.

Too many times people try to produce something without a solid foundation, just as we did with our first New Mexico gardening attempt. We hurriedly put up a small fence and planted some seeds in totally unprepared ground, knowing the probable results, but feeling the need to get in a garden. We were correct about the results, but the effort at least produced a conceptual capacity for what would be needed in the future. We were able to observe the seasonal sun path, temperature ranges, weather patterns, wilting heat, and the need for shade.

After some basic steps for the garden were taken, the soil was tested, and nutrients were added, we sought embellishments that both fit in with the environment and were beneficial to the garden.

One element was the building of small pools with re-circulating water, which drew birds, bees, toads, and other beneficial wildlife. Then, looking around for something to provide both shade and what we like to call "vertical interest," we inspected one of the telephone poles and were amazed to discover they were western red cedar. Since we had built raised beds, trellises, and pea poles from western red cedar on San Juan Island off the coast of Washington State, we realized we had a familiar material with which to work.

The concept of the thin pieces of trellis once being a large telephone pole never fails to interest those who come by to see the gardens, and always elicit questions as to how they were made.

By moving to New Mexico, our concept capacity had been enlarged by the use of building materials not used in other places we had lived, like adobe and straw bale construction. When we began to consider building a strawbale wall around the front of the house to keep out the spring winds, creating a microclimate, and retaining some warmth in winter, adobe was a first thought. But our property had only sand, no clay for adobe bricks.

We thought back to the gardens we had built when we moved from San Juan Island to Arizona, where there was only hard, sticky clay. In the Pacific Northwest, there was an abundance of fertile sandy soil, so we tended to view the clay as a detriment. We dug out some of the Arizona clay and built fieldstone raised beds on top of it, added organic matter, composted manure, gypsum, and other nutrients to the beds, and after three years we had fertile soil.

If, instead, we had moved to Arizona from New Mexico, we would have rejoiced at the valuable clay material that was in abundance. We could have used it to make adobe brick for walls, raised beds, out buildings, and housing.

So, here we were in New Mexico, with the concept capacity for adobe, but little of the material in our area. We had fine sand, which had, over time, leached out every possible nutrient.

One of the aspects of using adobe in a southwest climate is that it handles extremes, keeping cool in summer yet maintaining warmth in winter. Another building method and material used, with many of the same properties as adobe, is strawbale construction.

We built a strawbale wall around part of our house that provided us with a microclimate for an enclosed garden (the temperature inside this wall was ten degrees warmer year around). We used three of the higher wall corners to incorporate a cedar pergola to shade the seating area underneath, adapting the cedar rails much like the Navajos use willows for shade over their summer outside cooking area called a "chaha'oh."

In an attempt to enlarge the conceptual capacities of others, and ourselves we dedicated the second half of one of our sustainable organic gardening workshops to a broadening exploration into other viewpoints. For example, at one organic gardening workshop, we had two artists and a poet, each providing a new avenue of viewing and perspective of what had been created in the gardens.

For one of the fall gardening workshops we were fortunate to have had a guest speaker who lived and worked in the "waffle" gardens with her grandmother in an abandoned Zuni village that was last occupied in the 1950s (hopefully someday to be restored).

We hoped that this information would provide trellising for incorporating a greater understanding of cultural "whys and wherefores," because progress goes forward when individuals seek out, implement, and share their concepts and ideas.

Personal gardening progress is impeded by agribusiness, which provides the majority of food most people eat, and establishes a mediocrity by eliminating biodiversity, creating a petro-chemical dependency, and interrupting the natural rhythms that regenerate and renew our resources.

Let each of our gardening endeavors reflect for others new concepts that will allow a natural progression toward a better planet on which we will all be able to grow.

Pink Columbine

VITAL VICISSITUDES
Building a Gateway

Even blessings require an exactitude. One year the warm weather and no late frosts had put the garden and the opening of the farmers market a month ahead of schedule. The mornings had been cool, even chilly, (twenty-six degrees one morning before sunrise), but readily warming as the sun topped the mesas and began its daily ascent.

In the afternoon, hot dry winds blew across the raised beds. Frost tender plants that would have been set outside already had fruit and blossoms. Being gardeners, we always tried to push the envelope of earliness, and that year was the earliest by far.

Every day ended the same; as the bright sun lowered to the western horizon, we entered the garden and watered. We had not had any rain to speak of in ninety days. At times, the clouds would gather and distant rumbling brought hope, but the brief storms passed us by as they skirted along the base of the Zuni Mountains to the north.

In July, the afternoon monsoons would hopefully appear, bringing afternoon clouds and rain, cooling and watering the garden with those ion rich drops that make plant colors glow with new growth. Until then, there was nothing we could do but water every day, sparingly on the spinach and heavy on the lettuce.

A strawbale workshop that year brought in people from all over New Mexico, some from Arizona, and one from Colorado. There were Navajos, Zunis, Hispanics, old and young (one in a stroller), students, and assorted locals. Our friend and co-presenter, "Preston of the Mojave" provided a wealth of knowledge, tools, experience, and a ready smile.

The project for the workshop was to build an entrance wall on each side of the driveway, and two walls of a small room with a framed window on each side. The rubble-filled foundations had already been poured, so when the "bookwork" was over, the stacking of the bales, cutting custom sized bales, and wiring the bales began. No one really knew what to expect, but all were charged with enthusiasm, and the spirit of creating something through cooperation.

After eating lunch in small groups, using the time to become better acquainted, the work continued. As the bales were stacked, wire was applied, cement was put on, and a change from nothing began to take a recognizable shape.

Everyone had driven in past the foundations that were near the ground showing only a few pieces of rebar sticking up. During those hours of the day, willingness became the watchword: "I'll go get it," and "Let me help with that" were commonly heard.

By late afternoon the combination of physical labor, long distances to drive home, and a consensus of knowing that we had done what we could, ended the workshop. After hugs, handshakes, exchanging addresses, business cards, and phone numbers, everyone went to their cars and drove out on the same road as they had come in. Only this time they left through an entry way they had helped to build, and were now going back to their pueblos, back to the reservations, back to the cities, back to their communities where they would give of their experiences to help others.

The *fin de siecle* of the twentieth century came and went with no seeing the "end of the world as we know it" (Y2K). No returning Messiahs, or any global realizations of world peace through Harmonic Convergences of people or planets aligning. That *tertium quid* of expectation remained sought after, expected, called upon, given up on.

There are vicissitudes that will come surely as the morning sun; some will try to force their arrival with political ballots or bullets. Others, numbed by money, media, and megabytes don't care. Meanwhile our garden needed watering until those afternoon clouds might build, darken, and give us that much-needed rain.

Gateways show a port of entry into possibilities where other factors are applied, and opportunities for change can sprout when given the needed nutrients. As we head toward a greater global cooperation, the fact remains that we have to go through those gateways and water until that time when those vital vicissitudes sprout and we can truly begin to grow.

Wild New Mexico Primrose

Dandelion

PRAXIS RELAXES

At an altitude of 7,300 feet, summer always arrived suddenly, like an unannounced visitor, leaving us scrambling to plant and transplant, pick up, straighten up, and generally make presentable the garden, greenhouse, and yard.

Plants that seemed to be doing fine in their four-inch pots only a couple of days ago clamored to be relocated to new homes where their roots would be unconfined. They were eager to burst forth with new growth and their promise of bounty.

All the plants grown inside the small greenhouse had been taken to their "staging area" just outside the large vegetable garden next to a second greenhouse that provided a sheltered haven in the event of a surprise frost (which could easily happen into June). Plants transplanted into freshly tilled garden soil just seemed to explode overnight, and toads rushed into the ponds to mate.

It's not that we didn't know this was going to happen, we had been planning for it since we closed down the garden that past fall; it's just that there is an unexpected moment, a chasm leap from potential to entelechy that, however prepared for, always catches us in mid-step, causing a stuttering re-adjustment in our daily routines.

This is what we had been preparing for the last few months. It had been the when, the how many, and the how much that were the items of speculation. The preparation, it seemed, was always more challenging than the application.

We also had good weather for our recent rockwork workshop, the early morning sun and late morning clouds were perfect. Native American high school students came from Pine Hill and Zuni, a Navajo artist/teacher came all the way from Ganado, Arizona; people came from Albuquerque, Gallup, and the Ramah area. We walked and talked about rocks, designs, pools, ponds, and cement.

There were questions about tools, rock shaping, and techniques that kept everyone busy until lunch, the social aspects then taking over as we laughed and ate. Soon it was time to go from theory to praxis.

Everyone eagerly grabbed trowels, shovels, hoes, rock hammers and headed out to the chicken coop to do the next section of rock wall, building onto what the two previous workshops had built. Each person was ready to do something physical, something concrete, after so much "book learning" and information.

We showed them how to mix the first load of cement and then we went to work. Some wanted to work on a pad just outside the door going into the chicken run; others couldn't wait to start putting rocks in the wall, chipping and shaping, or filling the back of the wall with rubble and cement.

As with the other workshops, cooperation reigned: each took a turn with another person to mix the cement, shoveling in the three sand and one cement ratio, mixing it dry with the hoe, adding water slowly so it wouldn't be soupy, and then mixing until it was the same consistency as the demonstration batch.

Everyone was able to observe, help, and learn from each other. In a few hours all were ready to stand back and watch the magic transformation that occurs when the cement is struck (excess cement is removed), washed with a whisk broom and cleaned to reveal the shape of the rocks fitted in next to each other by the many eager hands.

Just like the rock wall, the previous year's garden received a new layer. The transition was being completed. Plants held back from frosts and freezes now had quarters in their allotted spaces. Strolling, weeding, and watering now provided a different tempo. Preparation had become praxis, and with it an end to the period of waiting, and the beginning of growing.

CHAORDIC-ADEPT ADAPTABILITY

Dee Hock was CEO of VISA International. He introduced principles, which enabled people and institutions to unite in a common goal in which members simultaneously engaged in the most intense cooperation and fierce competition. He coined a word from chaos and order, Chaord, meaning any self-organizing, self-governing, adaptive, non linear, complex organism, community or system, the behavior of which harmoniously blends characteristics of both chaos and order.

The gardener is *self-organizing*, there are no set rules as to when to start germinating seeds, what seeds to plant, how early to plant or by what methods. The gardener must be *self-governing*; no amount of wheedling, cajoling, or threats can make one go out and spend the time needed for a successful garden.

If nothing else, the gardener must be *adaptive*; the perfect garden of today can become an infested problem overnight, requiring inventiveness, resourcefulness, and the ability and knowledge to know and choose those measures needed to correct the situation.

Although the garden itself is indeed a linear affair, proceeding from germination to fruition, the actions taken to make this happen are *non linear*, as the gardener searches the possibilities each day in order to deal with a multitude of events happening in the garden's synergy.

The garden itself becomes a *complex organism*, a *community* and a *system*, involving family, neighbors, and in the case of food banks, farmers markets, community gardens, and co-ops, an ever-expanding radius of influence.

And, it is our behavior that "*harmoniously blends characteristics of both chaos and order.*" We can do this if we:

1. *Stay focused*—let a daily assessment give direction.

2. *Stay relaxed*—don't let problems that pop up frustrate to the point of, "I give up."

3. *Stay balanced*—emphasize common sense, keep things in proportion, and assimilate wholeness.

4. *Stay loyal*—get out to the garden every day, even though some days you may feel it doesn't need you, or you don't feel like it.

5. *Stay determined*—inexplicable crop failures, poor germina-

tion, insects, weather, or infestations can cause a wavering in dedication.

6. *Stay non-judgmental*—sometimes the solutions for problems are those you thought would never work.

7. *Stay driven*—the garden is not to be only for your pleasure and benefit; make it produce for others.

8. *Stay cooperative*—disseminate your product, your enthusiasm, and your knowledge.

A Chaord is characteristic of the fundamental organizing principles of evolution and nature. We believe these organizing principles to be Truth (facts), Beauty (ideas), and Goodness (relationships).

Everyone starts seeds at different times. For us, it wasn't by the *Old Farmer's Almanac*, or the weather, it was an intuition, an internal prodding that sprang up suddenly and urged us to "get things going."

We went into the greenhouse and leveled the spot where the one-inch thick piece of Styrofoam would rest, and placed our heating mat on it. We plugged it into the control panel on the wall, out of which spiraled a thermal sensor connected to the thermostat.

We went to the basement and filled five seed trays, seventy-two holes in each, with our seedling mixture, watered the trays in which they sat, and planted them all within a few hours. We had begun this year's adventure in "chaord gardening."

The seed catalogs we received each year gave us new varieties along with heritage seed from the past. Magazines touted new tools for weeding, seeding, and reading. It was up to us to be adept at adapting these new choices into our schemes.

Let us, through our gardens, discover Beauty in things, recognize Truth in meanings, and find Goodness in values. Then, we can grow.

FLUXION TO GRADE

One year, on the fourteenth of June at about two-thirty a.m. we woke up, knew it was cold, and walked out to the garden to check the thermometer: it read thirty-eight degrees F. We were expecting a light frost and the vulnerable plants in the garden were snuggled under a blanket of spun cloth used for frost protection. We closed the ends of the plastic garden greenhouse and secured them with cinder blocks, and went back to bed.

In the morning when we opened the gate and walked into the garden at five-thirty a.m., we could feel that something was wrong. We looked at the thermometer in the middle of the garden and it read twenty degrees. In three hours, it had dropped eighteen degrees.

The lettuce was frozen to the touch (one and a half weeks away from being sold at the farmers market) and the beans, corn, peas, and rhubarb, which we had covered with a triple layer of Remay (a spun cloth used for frost protection) were frozen solid. So were the, squash, tomato, and pepper transplants we had just put out two days before.

One of the great things about gardening is that there is a period of beginning and ending, each year being another repeated completion. We thought, this year we would have to have two beginnings. We waited as the sun came up, knowing that at the end of the day we would have a better idea of what the real damage was.

By evening, most of the lettuce leaves were black, the tomatoes entirely black as were the squash, and peppers, and even the peas were damaged. Freeze-burn-black seemed to pervade the garden that only yesterday had seemed so promising, so beautiful, so green. Perennials ready to burst open with flowers were black and limp.

Two weeks later, the garden began to get back into shape. The outer leaves of the lettuce had been removed and soon they were back to how they looked before the freeze. The corn had re-emerged with new tips from ground level, the rhubarb had sent up fresh new shoots, and the peas were sending out new runners. A few squash were producing new leaves with a vengeance, and the perennials had begun to recover. All in all, it was not as bad as it had first seemed.

Fluxion is the act of flowing, like water going downstream. At the top of our south ridge when it rained, the water started down the hill rapidly in a narrow stream and widened as it neared the bottom where it spread out until it reached "grade" or the place "so adjusted to conditions of slope, volume, and speed of water, that no gain or loss of sediment took place." The water ran its course from this rushing start to a final wide spreading stop.

In the garden it is much the same. Spring starts the activities with rushing and all kinds of preparation. The focus is narrow and hurried: bed preparation, mulching, seeding, transplanting, watering, weeding, and keeping a mindful eye on the weather.

We seemed to be somewhat down the hill now, broader in scope, yet still rushed along. In a streambed, immovable objects like large rocks (or hard frosts in the garden bed) were skirted around and their immovable natures better dealt with by a yielding hand.

Just as water goes to each side around an object, we took out what was dead, saved what we could, replaced what we had to, and rushed on, for we were in the midst of another "repeated completion," another year of going from seed to harvest, knowing the expectations of effort, skill, knowledge, inventiveness, focus, dedication, and decisions, that were needed to complete this cycle.

These were our fluxions, our acts of flowing, and at the end, we would arrive at garden grade, when all the harvest was in and put away and no more sediment was moved until spring. Without fluxion, we couldn't grow.

Russian Sage

GARDENING OURSELVES

Sitting on the front porch taking the rest of the afternoon off to relax, we once joked about how the garden was a fine place to "weed your brain." In the summer's hecticness of building and growing, outside intrusions can become buried in the mind like weed seeds from over the fence that are blown into the garden, and then days, weeks, or sometimes even next year, they pop up, surprising us with their impropriety.

Large and seemingly important events creep in through repetition or are headline blasted into our lives; T-cells, cloning, genetic re-combination, forcing us to take a side (and there always seems to be only two) on issues that for the moment are more abstract than present. The more complex society becomes, the more there is a need for protective habitual practices. In the garden, there is watering and weeding.

Lingerings of the 1960s "do your own thing" still color any ameliorative ideas of routine and habit. But perforce, the gardener must pursue them. The road to maturity in ourselves and in our plants showed that at first what we may have considered time consuming and irritating later proved most time saving and restful. These intervals of weeding and watering showed us what we could do, rather than what we couldn't do.

We were able to acquire and develop a skill that rose above inherited ability. Having a skill is a source of satisfaction in living, each individual finding their own niche somewhere in the garden: the reddest tomatoes, sweetest corn, the first peas, the longest carrots. Properly tending the garden allows one to be a producer as well as a consumer.

The daily-garden-walk-through-viewing made us face new realities (why weren't the beet seeds up after two weeks?) and adjust our ideals (of seeing those roundish purple globes) to the fact that they had been planted just right, covered just so, watered regularly, and now, this was no longer relative and needed to be "mind-weeded" to allow new directions and possibilities to enter and sprout. Incidents such as these are to our benefit: wisdom comes from adjustments made during the growing season.

It is great to have successes that can bring a smile of self-satisfaction and failures that allow us to learn to fail gracefully, using that disappointment to encourage us to try again in a different way, using new strategies.

When we first talked about growing artichokes at 7,300 feet in the New Mexico high desert, people sort of looked at us with blank stares. The first year we had an "okay" crop, not large, but showed us that it could be done. But, during the winter, they froze in the ground. The next winter we dug the roots out, packed them in sand in large pots, and put them in the basement, watering them only enough to keep them alive. In the spring, we re-planted them and had an early crop of "chokes" and another in late summer. The double crop was totally unexpected; our main concern had been simply to not have to start new plants each year. It was a great surprise for us.

Within the unknown there often pop up dividends. If we had not weeded our brain of the idea of a year-to-year starting of new plants, we would never have tried something new. Don't hesitate to discard and re-invent. Progress in the garden, and in ourselves, depends upon new opportunities for expression. Rodan of Alexandria said, "Many noble human impulses die because there is no one to hear their expression."

Fortunately, our gardens are always there listening, helping us to grow.

LIFE SCALES

Within our strawbale wall were formal gardens and two decorative rock pools; one was only about four-feet wide, the other eight-feet across. Although shallow, the eight-foot pool held a lot of water, the hot June winds blew across the top sucking the moisture into the air, and with the small jet of water spraying up from the re-circulating filter/fountain, it evaporated quickly.

Filling it was a daily process. This pool was also under a piñon tree and filled up with pine needles, blowing sand, and falling leaves from the three Silver Lace vines planted around it, and clogged the filter under the rocks where the goldfish loved to hide beneath and breed.

Traditionally, our monsoon weather arrived in July, bringing cool afternoon clouds, rain, and calm breezes. We had to make a choice. We could continue to put water into the pool daily, clean the pond and the filter more often, or fill in with dirt. Finally, our sensibility and conscience got the best of us and the goldfish were moved to the smaller pool, still able to hide under rocks and swim against the current from the fountain.

After we bailed out all of the water and used it to water surrounding plants, we sifted one of our compost piles and filled the pool space to the rim. One pile equaled the water removed, like some twisted Archimedean principle. This was another step taken in the new direction, which had begun with our decision to plant only half of the main garden.

When living on San Juan Island, off the coast of Washington State, we had formal gardens that were also open to the public, and often visitors would rave about them. We would ask them if they had been to the Butchart Gardens near Victoria, B.C. ten miles across the Straits of Juan De Fuca at the south end of Vancouver Island. They would often reply with, "Yes, but these gardens are much nicer."

For a long time we wondered why we received this response, having been to those world famous gardens that were created in an old limestone quarry and covered many acres. Then one day we discovered why: *scale*.

Remembering when we visited the Butchart Gardens, and walked around for the first time seeing hundreds, if not thousands, of plants in huge formal beds and themed gardens, it was overwhelming for us as gardeners to understand the machinations behind such an endeavor. We later found information about the large number of employees needed to create and maintain the gardens, which were more of a corporate expression, and therefore less intimate and personal.

At dinner with friends one night, we savored the taste of their first-of-the-season radishes, and each expressed an opinion as to the cause of a few that were "pithy." Was it too much water, not enough water, was it too hot, did a cold snap hit them?

If they had been from the supermarket, comments probably would not have been made, other than some disparaging remark about the store that sold them.

Globalization grows daily, creating a scale of interaction that affects us all. Scale (from the Latin, *scal*, meaning *ladder, stairs*) is a graduated series, a succession or progression of steps or degrees. It is corporate expression inexorably climbing that ladder of larger and more. Drought? Drill more wells, deeper.

Personal expression allows an individual the choice to go back down rungs, easing conflicts and adapting sensibly to situations that involve more than just one's self-interest.

Personal expression is more able and more apt to choose a proper ratio between self and events, a ratio that in the end will provide an account, a reckoning of actions showing that often by doing with less, we will have grown more.

THE DANCING HATCH

We often talk about situations in the garden in terms of condition (from the Latin, *condition,* meaning *to place in proper order*). Crowding can be a condition that will necessitate thinning or transplanting, re-arranging the plants for a more desirable spacing, one that will let each plant grow to its potential.

We also condition the garden by the manipulation of materials: compost, mulch, water, nutrients, weeding, seeds, and transplants.

To promote a more favorable condition requires purposive planning. In the same way as we expect a larger plant from proper spacing, we can expect and plan for other results from the desired order we establish. Hopefully, one of these factors of condition will be enjoyment.

When we build a new growing bed, we make them small enough to be able to work the middle without having to stand in the bed or stretch to the point where whatever we are doing is awkward or uncomfortable. Better to have a smaller bed that promotes working ease than one just a bit too large, growing frustration and a lack of enthusiasm at the thought of having to do battle with it all summer.

The overall garden view can give us relaxation, peace, and a sense of achievement, confidence and satisfaction. One condition that can hinder the desired effects is weeds. We have known gardeners who started a season full of enthusiasm and hope, and then allowed weeds to accumulate to the point that they dreaded going out to their garden. We preferred heavy mulching for control; weeds could not get enough light to germinate, and those that did were easily pulled out, and more importantly, easy to spot.

By promoting the right conditions, weeding can become a pleasant experience. Using a layer of mulch will provide a consistent background between each plant, and make it easier to re-adjust the eye focus to a different level of seeing: looking for the anomaly. Often this mental re-focusing led to small satori moments while walking and gazing, insights and sometimes solutions to other situations came into mind.

One day, when we had just sat down on a garden bench near the end of the day, the sun almost to the horizon, we looked to the west and saw a cloud had mostly covered the sun's horizontal rays, producing a diffused light that showed there was a new hatch of insects in the air, flying up as far as they could, falling downward, and then rising back up.

We thought of the times when we sat in a room and suddenly saw all the dust particles floating in the air, exposed by the light at just the right angle, or when we saw rays of light shooting from a cloud to the ground like stairs leading to heaven. A few moments later the chance conditions were different, and the dancing hatch disappeared from view.

We knew that there were hundreds of insects in our air even though we could no longer see them. Events like seeing a dancing hatch seldom occurred, but when they did, our knowledge and appreciation was increased.

Within the garden, we are able to promote opportunities by making conditions ripe, allowing us to harvest unseen fruits. Thank goodness for our gardens which help us to grow.

Heritage tomatoes

A SIMPLEX CONCERN

At twelve-forty-two a.m., lightning and thunder awoke us and the winds that had been blowing hard through the windows when we went to bed had now turned into a gentle quiet breeze. We could hear the raindrops on the deck outside, beginning with a few and then increasing in number until the sound of rain, the good, steady, not-too-much-at-once kind of rain, lulled us back to sleep.

In the morning, we could see the ground was dark and wet, not just dimpled from a brief few drops. New footprints trailed us in the sand on the way to the garden. This was the first rain we had had this season. Everything looked fresh and glowing, renewed by the ionized water that also gave that scent of wet dirt and desert grasses.

For the moment, we reveled in the simple sights and smells of the garden. By mid-afternoon, the hot sun had taken away all traces of the moisture that had been given. At the end of the day, we (again) watered the thirsty plants.

A friend from back east visited that summer, and told us about a project concerning the effect technology has had, and is having on, people. She didn't give any specifics as the project was not completed at that time, but she did hint that some of the effects found were "not good."

These studies were not of a scientific, data gathering nature, but rather derived from think-tank sessions in informal settings: a search for boundaries to encompass what is contained in this new Information Age, spawned by the Technological Age. It is the struggle to predict a paradigm.

It is the gardener who, still having one foot in the Agrarian Age, is able to layer the levels of progress and become a cohesive director of humankind's march to discover what that long ago planted seed of humanity will become.

The Industrial Age broadened and diluted our earth connection by use of chemicals and machines, leaving fewer and fewer people with a direct link to the most basic of all activities—working with the soil.

Information determines behavior and provides a dominant and fundamental way of thinking over a period of time. If it proves successful, this cycle forms a paradigm. At present we are in the formative stages of what to do with the information that is so abundant.

After seeing charts and data about *El Ninos* and *La Ninas*, global warming, and our own first-hand experience with this summer's heat and drought, we decided on a course of action toward our concern (from the Latin, *cernere*, meaning *to separate, sift*.) Our consideration wasn't derived from abstract causes of behavior or effects. Our most simplex concern was water, as important in the Agrarian Age as it is today in the emerging Information Age, yet often overlooked because of its fundamental nature.

Our solution to conserve water was to halve the large vegetable garden. We did not replant as usual after taking harvested produce to market. Our method was simple (from the Latin, *simples*, meaning *literally one-fold*.) By "folding" the garden in half, we saved half our water. This affected not only us, but also our neighbors, who, although they had wells at different levels were interconnected.

Most of the plants, especially the perennials, were taken out and planted in the formal garden area around our house. The strawbale wall surrounding it helped prevent water loss from the wind, and the large trees inside it provided shade protection from the sun. That one-half of the larger garden was then allowed to "return to nature."

There are many options available to help conserve water in the garden: high tech pellets that absorb multiple times their weight in moisture (but not approved for organic growing), reflective ground coverings, or shade cloth to reduce the heat. But all involve an uptake in other energies that only defer and delay the real need for doing with less.

The Information Age paradigm will not be formed by sitting in rooms filled with discussion. It will be formed by self-organizing individuals who can make a prediction and provide a solution that relies on an actual basis of existence, that firsthand experience that has been derived from the garden.

From Agrarian Age to Informational Age we can provide a conterminous practicality that if successful, can form a paradigm for the future. We won't talk it into being, we will grow it.

VIABLE VISIONS

The morning was sunny and warm and all was in readiness for the strawbale workshop. We had just bought thirteen old bales of oat hay that had been stacked outside leaning against the hand-hewn logs of a deteriorating barn. It took a while to get through the stack and find bales with both wires still attached, but finally we had enough for the project and a few more "just in case."

We were able to get them for one dollar a bale as opposed to bales that can cost from six to eight dollars. After we unloaded them at the project site, we re-tied them with bailing twine, making them more compact and stable for stacking.

Off to each side of our new driveway we had poured two cement foundation pads, six inches high, twenty inches wide and six feet long, filled with rubble rock, and a final layer of cement on top. Two pieces of re-bar had been pounded into the ground, sticking up through the smoothed cement to impale and hold in place the bottom layer of bales.

The project for the day was a tiered entryway of stacked, cemented straw bales, later to be color coated with a coat of stucco when the cement dried. There were two bales on the bottom layer, one bale and a half for the next course, and then one bale on the top, giving the New Mexico look of stair steps or, as it is sometimes known, "Santa Fe-ing."

Although there are many materials one can apply to the outside of the bales, we have found over the years that most people want something practical and convenient. All of the participants at the workshop had thought about and imagined enclosures they wanted to make. Some wanted a wall to keep out the noise from a road in front of their home. Another couple wanted to use it for horse fencing. Others wanted outbuildings or tool sheds. We assured them that each project was possible, and explained to them that we had once built a strawbale outhouse as one of our workshop projects.

After introductions and a brief talk on what the plan for the day was, we began. Once the bales were stacked in sequence, we wrapped them with stucco lath that was attached to the bales by making six-inch long "u-shaped" pins from old bailing wire. Then the pins were pushed through the lath into the hay until the lath was firmly pinned against the bales. Everyone took a turn using the wire cutters to make pins, keeping everyone busy.

Soon we had the first side covered. Then we mixed the special one-step cement called "Fastwall" which has small fibers in it to give it strength, prevent cracking, and to better hold the application of color coat, which would be applied when the cement had dried a few days.

We had many trowels and hawks (a flat metal square to hold cement with a handle underneath in the center) and everyone enjoyed trying their hand at applying the cement. While some participants were cementing the left side of the entrance, others began stacking the right side, putting on the lath, pinning it, and shaping the bales.

By noon, the sun, mixing cement, and applying the cement had taken its toll, and after the second structure was ready to cement, everyone pulled out lunches and sat around talking and eating. This was always one of the best parts of the workshops, eating together and talking about our progress.

Before each left that afternoon, they commented on the fact that that when they arrived there had just been a pile of materials and now there stood two walls, cemented, solid, and substantial. Each was confident that they could actually now bring into reality what they had envisioned. We have found that having a "hands-on experience" is the best impetus for the actual doing.

Visions are personal and defined only within the mind. How we form these mental images has long been debated. Plato, in his *Republic VII*, stated that we make mental images from the shadows of the real things in the world. Later, Bishop Berkeley defined his theory of idealism as mental images being equivalent to material reality itself. David Deutsch argues for a world that has a "real independent existence and that humans have successfully evolved by building up and adapting patterns of mental images to explain it."

To those adherents of scientific realism, mental images and the perception of them must be no more than brain-states. These brain-states maintain mental images as topographic and topological wholes.

Expression in the material world from the mental world allows us, as Wilhelm Von Humbolt says, "the infinite use of finite means."

Each year we combine the same finite elements of soil, water and seed into an infinite variety of shapes, colors, smells, and tastes. Each year, from within the mind's swirls, we bring forth a newness, which affirms the material fact that we can grow.

RECENT RETURNS

We first saw the holes when we took the dogs for their afternoon walk. They were about one-half inch in diameter and randomly scattered on the ground. As we kept walking, we saw more holes and recognized them as cicada exits. They begin their exodus in our New Mexico high desert area when the ground temperature exceeds approximately sixty-four degrees F.

Looking on the trunks of nearby piñon trees, we found numerous exoskeletons. After coming out of their holes, they climb up onto something that allows them to get a firm grasp for their molt to adulthood. We had found them, on not only trees and larger vegetation, but firmly stuck on the stucco of our house and on the strawbale wall.

They are not locusts, which are a type of grasshopper, but in the order *Hemiptera*, an order of true bugs that have a forewing thickened and leathery at the base, and membranous at the apex. Some believe the diaphanous wings are able to block ultraviolet rays.

There are two general categories of cicadas: the periodical, which have extremely long life cycles of thirteen or seventeen years, and the annual cicada species that we have in New Mexico, that remerge each year, having a two to eight year cycle.

The annual cicada are not as developmentally synchronized and therefore group emergence is not as great as the periodical cicadas, which can be as high as one and a half million per acre.

The males, once they molt, begin producing species-specific calling songs and congregate to establish aggregations that are sexually attractive to females. These songs, produced by special structures called tymbals, are found on the male's abdomen. A tymbal is also a kettledrum, an apt naming considering the din that comes from the numerous males seeking mates. Our annual chorus of males is not as loud as those greater emergences back east and in the north, where the periodical cicadas live.

While underground, cicada juveniles, called nymphs, suck root fluids for food and when above ground, adult cicadas feed on living woody vegetation with a piercing-and-sucking mouthpart just behind the forelegs.

Once mated, the females excavate a y-shaped egg nest in

living twigs, and lay up to twenty eggs. Six to ten weeks later, the first-instar nymphs drop from the trees, burrow underground, locate a rootlet for feeding, and remain there until their species timetable for re-emergence arrives.

One evening neighbors arrived for solstice, as they had at the equinox gathering, full of enthusiasm and good cheer. Although we all lived in relatively close proximity, everyone had been busy with his or her own projects; building a home, a garden, or repairing something as always seems needed when living in a rural area. After greetings and updates on what everyone had been busy at, we all gathered just after sunset in our newly constructed fire pit.

The sunken kiva-like fire pit was eight feet in diameter, and made from sandstone rock and cement. The seat, nineteen inches high with a sitting area nineteen inches wide, had an eight-inch backrest on one side made with four courses of old Gallup bricks scavenged from a farm dump, and huge flat limestone rocks on the other side. In the center was a round, sunken fire pit with a cooking rack.

As the longest day turned into the shortest night, we sat around the fire pit and read a short paper on solstice trivia. Others told stories of times of import in their lives, sharing humor and reflections. As was the case with most of these gatherings, the next event was eating. We had hot dogs made into our famous "butter dogs" by cutting them in half, barbequing them flat, and then topping them off with a layer of melted cheese. Accompanying them was a big potato salad, chips, assorted beverages, and brownies for dessert.

We sat talking, laughing, and roasting marshmallows, late into the evening as one of our truly talented neighbors played the guitar and sang. Later on, everyone strolled off into the cloudy, but moonlit night and headed home.

Periodic cicadas emerge at the same time each year because they have become "developmentally synchronized." Over a period of time re-association had set their internal clocks to sound the alarm to gather.

Our eyes and minds were watchful of the declining sun having passed its apex and would soon be reaching its autumnal equinox, sounding an alarm for us to again gather and share the developmentally synchronized aspects of our lives, celebrating and creating a horology that with each re-emergence would remind us that we had grown.

DEPENDENT INDEPENDENCE

The Fourth of July had arrived without a late June frost setting everything back. The Ramah Farmers Market was a week away, giving our produce more than a good chance to finish at peak growth. Although we were celebrating a day of independence, now was the time we also needed to express our dependence on each other.

We were depended upon to show up at the farmers market every weekend, at the same time, and with a good supply of fresh, organic vegetables for those wishing to exercise some "independence" from the chain markets in the cities.

So many times being dependent is seen as a fault or a weakness, and being co-dependent is thought to be even worse. But in this situation creating dependence is of great value, especially when we think of "dependence" as confidence, reliance, trust, and promoting the common good.

At the market, our buyers had confidence that they were getting organically grown, fresh picked produce. We generally picked for the market early the same morning, starting before the sun was up, the produce washed and placed in containers for the trip to town. Freshness is often one aspect of food that is overlooked, other than checking the "Best when used by . . . " expiration date. Buying fresh has many advantages: it has more nutritional value, keeps longer, looks and tastes better.

A mutual reliance and constancy was established at the market. Those who came each week relied on us to provide them with the ingredients with which to make again that great tasting salad they had the week before, and now wanted to have again. We relied on them for our summer income.

One method we used to maintain consistency was to grow small crops using high rotation. Planting became part of the periodic rhythm of the garden's summer life. Seed trays, with seventy-two planting holes were continually seeded to provide backup plants in case of late frosts, or sudden hailstorms that shredded the plants, or for use as immediate transplants to replace those picked and taken to market.

This method took less garden space, saved time, used fewer nutrients, and allowed for intensive companion planting when transplanted. Seedling trays used much less water, a big factor in our area, since we were experiencing the severest drought in one-hundred years.

Trust is essential for a successful garden. The plants unthinkingly trusted that we would water them, feed them, and help them attain their optimum fruition. We trusted that our efforts would bring forth successful results, and that people would come to the market.

The Fourth of July is a holiday celebrating independence—breaking away from our daily paths, suspending our regular systems, and gathering with friends, neighbors, and family, in whom we had confidence and trust that allowed us just to enjoy being ourselves.

In parks, campgrounds, and other areas where there are celebrations of independence there is also reliance upon each other—a holiday dependency promoting a common good. Independence is strengthened in and by each person, and as goes one, so goes the whole, and we grow.

A rock wall raised bed "welcome"

WHEN THE SEASON?

The expenditure of time and effort in the garden is payment in and of itself, and the actual harvest becomes a bonus paid for diligence. Other rewards that accrue range from financial to altruistic; the financial side rarely amounts to a full repayment, especially when one considers the number of hours dedicated to planning, preparing, and pampering a garden, whereas the altruistic returns are gathered on the inside, safe from inflation and theft.

It is natural to want to protect one's investment, to make sure that the worry, the sweat, and the results are used in the most economic and practical way possible, thus keeping in step with the original creation of the goods. Any abundance must be dealt with in an expeditious manner lest weather, age, or animals destroy it before its allotted purpose is fulfilled.

If there is a farmers market nearby, buyers attending always appreciate the greater selection provided. Most neighbors and friends enjoy food given to them freely, their appreciation deepened by their knowledge of your enterprise and dedication.

It is not strange or difficult to believe that sharing is an aspect of universal economy. Within each person, there is the need for a proper intent of identity expression. Donating to a food bank allows one to be charitable. Having delivered the food, one can be allowed a sigh of satisfaction knowing that we have at least in some measure, given back, or created an allocation for someone other than ourselves. It is up to the individual to determine his personally required quota (from the Latin, *quota pars*, meaning *how great a part*).

When our gardens were larger, we tended to plant a lot of kale. Most people only know kale as that vile tasting, tough, and unappealing vegetable matter used as a garnish. Kale is one of those vegetables better eaten freshly picked, since toughness and bitterness occurred within a few days of harvest.

Kale was always one of the last items left on our table at the farmers market, even after offering it free and extolling its virtues of having antioxidant properties and great vitamin C content, most said, "No, thank you." When there was no one else to sell or give it to, the compost welcomed it, providing excellent nutrients for next year's crops. However, when we added it to our prepared salad mix, people began to realize how good it was if fresh.

Religious organizations and societies usually fed the less fortunate throughout history. In biblical times, gleaning was an honored method, allowing the hungry to gather whatever grains were left in fields after a harvest. In the 1960s a new social conscious connection with food was publicized in the media, reporting on a group in San Francisco called the "Diggers" who fed hippies and the homeless.

An extreme form of urban gleaning grew with a group called the "Freegans." They included dumpster diving and foraging in city parks where edibles, unknown to most grew, like sorrel, bay leaves, or the wild parsnips in Brookland's Prospect Park. A less radical group called "Second Harvest" also made use of surplus and throwaway food to feed those in need.

There is a certain ignorant uncaring that develops when one has not put his "hand to the plowshare," as it were, as to the real value of food. Humankind suffered through a season of insecurity before agriculture established a winter surplus. Then a season of sufficiency and increase was given through science, and now, there is a season of abundance that is often misdirected and squandered, along with throwaway plastic that wrapped, transported, and displayed out of season produce from distant countries where its own inhabitants often starved for these same items.

We look for a new season of conscience, when one eats one's fill and then allots the rest to those in need. When that time arrives, we will know we have grown.

AUTUMN

*"The glory of gardening: hands in the dirt,
head in the sun, heart with nature.
To nurture a garden is to feed not just the body,
but the soul. Share the botanical bliss of gardeners
through the ages, who have cultivated philosophies
to apply to their own—and our own—lives:
Show me your garden and I shall tell you what you are."*

Alfred Austin, 1835-1913

The rewards of abundance

RAISING A GUEST NEST

It seemed as if the pace of daily life quickened this time of year. There was much to do, cleaning up debris, and checking again on the woodpile to evaluate the coming winter's toll.

Warm days allowed clear sailing through a list of "needs to be done" but there was that feeling of winter drifting in the wind telling us that we were at the edge of dropping off into to a deeper, freezing chasm that wouldn't thaw until spring.

We attended another Ramah Farmers Market's annual seed exchange/potluck. As in years past, there were free seeds, many saved by local gardeners from heritage varieties known to perform well in this area. There were message boards with photographs of people's gardens, some spoke about their garden, and on tables were lists and pamphlets about composting, and other literature of local gardening interest.

Almost everyone there was involved someway with the farmers market. Speakers ranged from a couple who grew specifically for the market, to those who grew medium to small gardens. We spoke about our GreenzBox™ (a self-contained raised bed four foot by eight foot growing box covered with shade cloth) how simple it was to do, and how effective it was for high altitude gardening.

A couple from Albuquerque liked the idea because they didn't know where all their utility lines were buried, didn't want to take a chance digging below ground, and were excited about being able to build it on top of the ground.

Another thing on our list was to start building a little "guest nest" a few hundred feet away from the hogan. We had already begun the project and we were expecting the arrival of some dear friends whom we hadn't seen in a couple of years.

We had just framed and sheathed the first wall when we heard the crunch of car tires on the gravel. We nailed as fast as we could, but were three nails short of completion when they pulled into the driveway and stopped in front of us.

We had been working hard, so this interlude with friends was well timed. We all sat around, talking and reminiscing, and had a great organic dinner with a salad of kale, spinach, chard and lettuce, then turkey, cranberry sauce, dressing, mashed potatoes and gravy, and ended with a rhubarb pie for dessert.

The next morning we met at an eatery a few miles down the road for breakfast, climbed to the top of El Morro, a nearby national monument, and peered down into walled rooms that were home to over eleven-hundred Anazazi more than eight-hundred years ago.

In the distance, from the very top of the monument, looking to the west, we could make out where our hogan was on the edge of a tree line. We descended and went back home. We put in the final three nails after we returned; the wall was now ready for raising. We had raised it by ourselves off the floor a bit earlier, but could feel by the weight that we would need an extra hand or two. With all hands lifting, the wall stood upright, was nailed, and secured.

It was only after we had hugged and waved goodbye that the experience the four of us had shared in raising the first wall of the guest nest stirred us. Echoes of pioneers working together in cooperation gave a quality to a simple act that, had we done it alone, would have been lacking.

Like the beginning leaves on a new seedling sprout, this first wall symbolized a potential for the future of those who would visit.

Around the world walls of exclusion have been erected by hands all too willing to help create division. Instead, let our hands help put up walls of welcome for those who seek unity.

Segmentation and separation will not bring forth the fruits of spirit. It will be by sharing our seeds of knowledge planted deep within the heart that will eventuate into a crop of guest nests that will grow.

SUBLIMATING VAPOR

The clean, evenly cut firewood was stacked neatly in-between four metal t-posts, two on each end, set about sixteen inches apart. There were glances of appreciation given by those whom we were visiting. Earlier that morning, we too had cut and split some juniper and stacked it on the porch near the front door.

People's woodpiles increase with the heaviness of the morning's frost. In the winter design, firewood is a local motif, the first of the many that develop as the cold progresses.

Being used, and reused, juniper fence posts have a longevity of usefulness. We had taken apart the old and rebuilt a new coyote fence made from the juniper posts previously used as a windbreak at our old garden site. We rebuilt the fence to define a new parking area, and create a safety barrier for a drop off. It also created a backdrop for new gardens planted behind it.

Wood comes into play even more in our lives as we had just finished a sixteen by twenty foot carport, built with split, western red cedar—old telephone poles that were used years ago before the milled and treated pine poles now being used.

We had a twenty by forty foot tarp we had previously used to cover firewood, so we were able to go over the top of the carport and cover two of the sides. The overhanging sides were rolled up around battens and nailed to the poles along the bottom. The carport prevented frost on the car windshield that got harder to scrape off, as the mornings got colder.

Even though we had several low temperatures around nineteen degrees F., we still had greens, herbs, and hardy perennials growing in beds that had been lined with thick stones that absorbed the heat during the day and radiated enough heat at night to prevent frost damage.

Frost is formed when water vapor goes directly from a vaporous state to a solid state. This process is called sublimation, and depends upon the loss rate of energy. Water vapor is in a higher energy state than liquid water, and liquid water is in a higher energy state than solid water (ice).

These different stages of cooling are called the dew point temperature (when the temperature is above freezing), and the frost point temperature (when the temperature is below freezing). The amount of moisture in the air determines when condensation, or sublimation, will be produced.

Black frost is formed when the temperature falls below freezing after dew has formed. Two other types of frost are rime and hoar. Rime frost is common during fogs, where super-cooled air comes in contact with subfreezing surfaces. This form of frost is opaque and has a grainy appearance that forms spikes, or needles. It does not have a recognizable crystal structure and is harder and denser than hoar frost.

Hoar frost generally forms when winds are light and the night is clear and cold. Growing from an initial seed of ice, hoar frost gives us the shapes of feathers, ferns, or flower patterns that we are most familiar with, especially in non-mountainous areas. It forms first on glass and metal surfaces, materials that radiate heat quickly and therefore cool quickly.

When frost begins to spread to the ground, it starts in the lowest regions. Once ice crystals have formed, further frost accumulation may proceed when the temperatures are colder and water vapor is deposited directly on a surface through a process called deposition.

A.N. Whitehead wrote that, "Life is an offensive, directed against the repetitious mechanisms of the universe." Just as frost surrounds us in potential, waiting for the right conditions to sublimate and appear in a changed form, so do we exist in a climate of expectation, waiting for conditions that will, once ripe, bring about higher aspirations.

And someday, like the hoar frost that appears suddenly, we will change the state in which we live, spread across the land, and grow.

GARDENING THE UNUS MUNDUS

One year, our first frost descended on September eighteenth, and was followed by four successive nights of early morning temperatures below twenty-eight degrees. The zucchinis we could not eat enough of suddenly were no more a problem with their now blackened, crisp leaves, so we harvested the last of their small fruits. The cayenne peppers in among the herbs and flowers were picked and the remains of the plants were pulled up for the compost bin.

Growing in large pots on the deck were cucumbers climbing up one of the posts, tomatoes, and Poblano peppers. They also were blackened. We removed them from the deck, harvested the rest of their fruits, and set the pots aside.

The shade cloth covering our raised bed box kept the frost from settling on the salad greens inside it. Knowing that only colder weather was in the future, we harvested large bags of greens for friends, and still had plenty left for salads and steamed greens.

The most interesting aspect of the year's gardening in the GreenzBox™ was the growth of spinach. During the annual Ramah Area Garden Tour in July, we had shown our spinach plants to one of our accomplished local gardeners. We noted how big the leaves were, and that they were the same plants we had put in the GreenzBox™ in the spring. The shade cloth had prevented them from bolting, (growing and immediately going to seed.) In New Mexico, spinach is one of the first plants to bolt in the hot sun, and yet we were still picking spinach from our original plants late into the fall.

To help formalize the fish pond we made a terraced raised bed on one of the side pond, filled it with compost and planted catmint, a drought resistant perennial which grew exceedingly well in this area.

Because of construction time constraints, the soil in the first perennial beds, interspersed culinary herbs and perennial flowers, had not been amended. But, as with most first year gardens, there were enough nutrients in the native soil to make things grow well. In one of the beds, we dug deep holes and planted rhubarb in a mixture of steer manure and potting soil.

When we emptied the large plastic pots we used for growing the peppers, cucumbers, and tomatoes on the deck, their roots were holding the organic potting soil tightly together. While we were trying to use a knife to break them apart, the blade went down through and a nice even slice separated and fell off. Since they were too difficult to crumble apart with our hands, we decided to cut them into slices about two-inches thick, starting at the bottom, working toward the tops. We cut some of the rounds in half and placed them around the edges of the beds, scalloped-like, with their flat sides out, thus providing an edge for water containment and mulch.

By recycling the soil and roots, which would break down during the winter, we liked to think we were on the edge of practicality.

The manifestation of unconscious products within a conscious activity is an element of spontaneity, and in this situation, the slices were an example of synchronicity.

Victor Mansfield points out that in Jungian synchronicity, such events bridge psyche and matter, the garden and the unus mundas, wherein, "synchronicity experience, meaning is the critical point."

Inasmuch as we needed more soil, the slices became a form of acausal orderedness, given to us from the unus mundas—the domain of unified potentiality—the collective unconsciousness.

There is a creative application in planting a seed, one that reaches beyond us as personal beings. The life germ that awakens and presents itself as a sprout, gives us an integrative knowledge that deepens our capacities for consciousness.

The garden exhibits and avails principles accessible to everyone as a collective understanding of the worlds we share.

There is a reality that hovers over surface events. It is incubated in the mind and birthed by our own hands into an experience that sends roots deep into an unexplored ocean of energy that will someday feed and transform a world that we will grow.

COMMONUNITY

One day we were asked to contribute one sentence for a magazine about how we felt toward a local intentional community (from the Latin, *commum* meaning *serviceable*) a group of people living together and sharing the daily chores, etc. The limitation made us think hard as to what we really felt and what the results of an eight-year long relationship with them were. A community is a work of art, including a wide range of diverse elements making the work a living and progressive organism moving toward group ideals.

Community is created by individuals who associate and strive for the betterment of the lives of its members. Exclusion of any element leaves the goal incomplete, lacking fulfillment of each individual's dreams. The larger the element left out, the fewer the fulfilling aspects.

In our area of New Mexico, we live in a predominately juniper-piñon tree community, along with Ponderosa pine at the higher altitudes. One seldom finds a piñon or a juniper growing alone. Generally they grow touching, within each other's branches. Their tenaciousness evidenced by trees growing out of the thinnest of cracks in sandstone or in lava fingers that had crept out from volcanic vents miles away.

Down the road to the east of us is the El Malpais National Monument. The early Spanish explorers named it El Malpais, or "The Bad Country." It has also been called a poor man's Hawaii because of all the various types of lava that can be found. Here too grow piñon and juniper, sending roots deep into lava cracks.

This El Malpais area is also one of the top five tree-ring sites in the world; the oldest Rocky Mountain Douglas Fir was found growing there. It sprouted in the year 1062, four years before the Norman Invasion of England.

A sub-community within the piñon -juniper is the Gambel Oak. Gambel Oak and Gambel Quail were named after William Gambell, a naturalist and ornithologist. These oaks range from 4,500 to 7,500 feet and are often found mixed in with Ponderosa pine. The acorns, a food source for indigenous peoples for thousands of years, are high in protein, carbohydrates, and calcium. Since oak trees hybridize in nature, new species are often discovered.

At the beginning of fall, when in other parts of the country leaves of deciduous trees are losing their green and changing to reds, yellows, purples, and oranges, the oak leaves at this altitude just turn a yellow/brownish color.

When the sun begins its decline, and the temperatures drop below freezing, a signal is sent to the tree telling it that it is time to stop producing chlorophyll, allowing a blend of pigments that have been present and patient all year, carotene and xanthophyll, to be activated. This results in the changing leaf color, and reduces the need for water during the winter months.

Our larger community, enriched by the many sub-communities following the seasons, hybridizing, and carrying forward traits and roots from an ancient time, push deep into the social bedrock, and once secure, will grow.

A perennial vine growing up a cedar trellis

RESIDENTS RESONANCE

One night we attended a friend's evening of performance art. It began with a defining rhythm beaten out on a large cottonwood bass drum using double drumsticks.

There were costumes, poetry, humor, philosophy, spirituality, and music. Seating was on floor pillows, couches, and chairs placed in front of a carefully designed set, lighted to set it apart from the rest of the room. This performance synchronized the evening with conviviality and cake.

Entrainment happens when the vibrations of one person cause the vibrations of another person to oscillate at the same rate.

Specialization in society has fragmented the perception of a personal effectiveness by making the individual a member of an ever-diminishing coterie, much in the same way as a gardener can only feed a few people at a local farmers market as opposed to the many that pass through a supermarket.

Aside from the taste, freshness, and the nutrition of locally grown food, there is an economy of resources that is passed on to those in the immediate area, as well as to those living miles away.

According to the Worldwatch Institute, an American meal travels an average of two-thousand miles or more, from farm to plate. This means that the average consumer, by eating one month's worth of meals, has had his food shipped the equivalent of going around the equator twice. The more markets provide foods that are "out of season" and from all over the world, the greater the use and pollution of the world's resources.

This complexity usually leads to thoughts of "overpopulation," and "how can we possibly feed more people?" Lavish fresh food displays contain more than can be bought, the rest ending up in dumpsters, thrown away, not recycled or given to those in need.

People complain about the high price of gas not realizing their evening meal has helped to create that high price.

Our bodies contain around forty billion cells. We tend to think of the brain as the leader of the body, when in fact, it is the brain that coordinates the needs of the body. When our cells need food, our brain directs our body to eat. We as individuals do not consciously decide to "be hungry."

Awareness of our body's needs is produced through cell

membranes as electromagnetic pulses, read by the brain, and then action taken to satisfy that need.

In 1952, W.O. Schumann discovered the existence of ELF (extremely low frequency) signals that pulsate in the cavity between the earth's crust and the ionosphere. He fixed the most predominant wave frequency at about 7.8 Hertz. These pulsations today are knows as Schumann Resonances.

EEG studies have shown that when a person is deeply relaxed, brain sine-wave patterns and the heart/aorta resonate in the 7.8 Hertz range.

Alpha waves (7.12 Hertz) are generated by the brain during dreaming and light meditation. As more neurons spread over the cortex, they bring calm, inner awareness, and learning. When we intentionally create alpha waves, we become environmentally synchronistic with a wave level that circles the earth.

The Schumann Resonance charge that circumnavigates the earth between the walls of the earth's crust and the ionosphere is created from the hundred or so lightning bolts that occur each second in the thousands of lightening storms that cover the earth every day.

We are connected to this electromagnetic highway when we participate in harmonious thoughts, just as a conductor leads an orchestra performance, creating rhythms and direction for an audience.

The realization of this connecting pathway can reinforce one's sense of effectiveness by knowing that, without even leaving our area, we can join and grow.

California Poppy

A BRICOLAGE MIND

Mind is just about all we have that is truly subject to our will, but that which we can imagine, picture in our head, never quite gets replicated in physical reality. We may get close, a satisfying approximation, an acceptable verisimilitude, but in the end, there are portions missing from the total. So we work with what we have at hand to bring about what we envision.

Ansel Adams said that, "Accidents happen to the prepared." No one wants to have an "accident" but all the time we have "accidental" events in our lives. Bits of information are presented to us over the radio, television, newspapers, the internet, and through those with whom we have a daily contact.

Are we prepared for this accidental (happening by chance) information? When it intersects with our lives, can or do we make use of it?

One weekend at another of our strawbale wall workshops, twenty people showed up ready to act on whatever information came to them and then, use it for a common project: a strawbale wall.

As with other workshops, we had a wonderfully diverse group. This time there were Zuni high schoolers, and a couple from Albuquerque who had been to two of the previous workshops (organic gardening and basic rockwork) so they seemed like old friends. There was a family with a young teen, also from Albuquerque, and a woman from Jamaica, who lived in the Zuni pueblo. She had also been to the previous workshops, creating an even larger family feeling. There were locals, two of whom had also been to previous workshops, and a Navajo man from Gallup who built and restored hogans.

All that most people need to strike out on their own on a project is a chance to have a directed hands-on experience. This time our project was to attach a five-foot tall strawbale wall to a rock wall at the base of our house. It would connect a gate opening to the two-hundred-forty-foot strawbale wall that ran around the front of the house. We had already poured a six-inch deep rubble foundation, leaving the forms in place for demonstration.

After discussing the importance of scale and grade, we stripped the forms from the foundation and went to work. The first two bales were set on rebar sticking up from the foundation, driven down into the earth and encased in the cement to stabilize the first row of bales.

The next course of bales were re-tied and customized in length to break with the bottom pattern and span the two, like brickwork. After the top course had been set, we began to put on stucco lath. We could have used stucco netting or chicken wire, but we find that stucco lath is easier for the novice to use when applying the "mud" or cement.

The lath was attached to the bales by cutting old bailing wire (ubiquitous in this part of the country) to make simple "u-shaped" pins that were pushed through the lath into the bales, securing them. By noon, the bales had become a metal lath monolith. We still had lots to do, so lunch was only a half hour.

There are various materials that one can use to put on the straw, such as adobe mud (clay and straw), or a lime plaster. We preferred to use a Portland cement/fiberglass mixture called "Fastwall." It was specifically designed to be used as a two-step process, covered with a stucco color coat, as opposed to the traditional three-step process—a cement scratch coat, a second cement coat, and then the stucco color coat.

We mixed the first batch of cement in the wheelbarrow and started on the top. Each person soon developed a method and style of application, each valid in its own way, and progressed toward the final total covering of the wall.

Not being used to the body motions needed for applying cement, everyone was tired and ready to step back and admire the combined effort when the wall was finished. We all gained a satisfaction at seeing something of substance standing solid where a few hours before there had been only empty space.

During construction "accidents" continually occurred, and were met with prepared minds that used those events and actions to build, "bricolage style"(from the French, *bricoler*, meaning *construction by whatever comes to hand style*) which became knowledge for their use at a later date.

We had all used "what was at hand" to construct a common reality that showed not only could we build together, we could grow together.

GOOD GROVES

Inside the strawbale wall around our house, there were two groves of piñon pine (Pinus edulis) about thirty-feet tall. They were probably around one-hundred-eighty years old. There were four in one grove and six in the other. We had trimmed the branches of their trunks up to about eight feet.

After cutting a limb, sap oozed for a couple of years looking like white Karo syrup poured in the winter. Sometimes globs of resin formed and fell on the ground, and later, when buffeted around in the sand by water and wind became round brown pearls of various sizes. When scratched or rubbed, the smell of piñon pine pitch was released.

Beneath the piñon groves, encircling rock beds were filled with hardy perennial plants, herbs, and flowers. Flat sandstone rocks pointed upward at the base of each tree held the soil away from the trunk, directing water to the original ground level of the tree.

The treetops were full and provided us with much appreciated shade in the summer, cooling the garden and house. Over the years we had used the twigs and trimmed branches for kindling. Our cats climbed the trees as getaways when one of them wanted another to "get away."

On one of the limbs there was a robin's nest that was re-occupied each year. We often watched them as they dropped from the nesting area down to a small decorative pool with splashing water, where they bobbed up and down, drinking from the pool and bathed in the warmth of the sun.

Our groves were a windfall, an unexpected gain, and a piece of good fortune. They were left standing when the other trees all around them were cleared for more pastureland. A windfall is also something blown down to the ground by the wind, such as a fruit.

While walking back and forth from our front gate to the porch each day, we kept watch in the gravel for oval, dark brown, piñon nuts. Periodically they dropped to the ground, especially when the wind blew and the cones were shaken, freeing the seeds. Often they were easy to spot on the gravel path, or in the garden beds on the carpet of green sedum, or the Woolly thyme.

The wildcrafting of piñon nuts provided supplementary income for the natives who sold them at the local trading post or to roadside buyers that posted the latest price-per-pound on a large piece of cardboard. Flour sacks and burlap bags were favorite containers. Some picked nut-by-nut off the ground while others spread blankets underneath the trees and hit the limbs with sticks, knocking the nuts out of the cones.

Piñon trees have been around for at least ten-thousand years, and maybe since the last ice age. They start bearing cones at about thirty-five years of age, and begin producing good seed crops at around one-hundred years, not hitting maximum production until they are around one-hundred-eighty years old. Some live a thousand years.

When a piñon cone receives the pollen blown from other trees, it closes up and begins to grow seeds that take four years to mature and become edible. They are high in zinc and their shells can be crushed and added to coffee adding a unique piñon flavor.

Often we gain a sense of time from the food we eat: we speak of "fast food," "quick snacks," and "eating on the run." From our garden, we eat one or two years of a crop, depending upon whether it is an annual or a bi-annual plant. Thus eating instills a property of time consciousness and growth.

When harvesting and consuming piñon nuts, we became aware of an "eating of the ages" and with the returning to a more natural food source, we gained an insight which would help guide us as we grew ever more rapidly, toward that *Mysterium Tremendium*, the tremendous mystery, of our own final flowering.

A goldfish pond surrounded by catmint

A PASSED FUTURE

We ended our participation at the local farmers market early one year because of the drought conditions in our area. We didn't replant every two weeks as we had in the past. The one soaking rain we received that summer was in September, too late to do anything but provide a short growth spurt for the remaining lettuce, kale, carrots, beets, peppers and squash, and a couple of days respite from our evening watering.

As night temperatures continued to drop, the speculation of an early frost was voiced in local conversations. The chilling freezes were only a few weeks away, but for us the season was officially over. We had beets, peppers, squash, and carrots to eat during winter, snow peas, greens, and small tender zucchini, salads with the fresh spinach, kale, and cucumbers from the greenhouse.

The ripening tomatoes were being "sun dried" for our winter pizzas. We had been enjoying the textures of our seven varieties of kale, which would be the last things standing before the winter cold took them, and spring waited in the future.

We went to a bar mitzvah where the rabbi reminded everyone how the ceremony had been passed down and performed for the last three thousand years, and that today, history and tradition connected and continued to become a building block in the foundation upon which our neighbor's son might someday watch his son participate in the remembrance and re-enactment of becoming a "Son of the Commandment," an adult in the affairs of the world.

We joyfully entered into the spirit and symbolism of the event, the men wearing the yarmulkes provided. Even though this rite of passage, when a boy becomes a man, was spoken in Hebrew and the customs were unfamiliar for us, it cut across all language, cultural, and personal-belief barriers to address what it meant to take on the responsibilities of making the world a better place, leaving behind that innocence given as a privilege of youth.

Then, for the rest of the afternoon, we feasted and danced in celebration of the addition of one more person who would be giving his energies to provide our small community, and the world, a new and greater vision for our future.

Vernor Vinge speaks of *Singularity*, a future event in history at which time technological progress accelerates beyond the ability of current-day human beings to understand it.

Another definition proposes that *Singularity* is the culmination of some telescoping process taking place in the universe since the beginning of human civilization, or even before life on earth.

If and when this event occurs, humankind's new vestments will be sewn with the threads of repeated knowledge, allowing all to join in a rite of passage from innocent irresponsibility to a brother/sisterhood of new ideals, and we will grow.

Chamomile near the garden pond

A PREPONDERANCE OF CHANCE

As another month passed, the morning temperatures were noticeably cooler when leaving the house in the morning, slipping down into the twenties. Each plant had its tolerance level and showed the dead blackness when reached.

The summer chores of planting and putting in were now replaced with snipping off and pulling out, lessening the visible green and exposing more of the brown earth, not seen since last winter.

Unfinished projects became more evident. A winter pace had been set, slower and more methodical than the lively planting jig danced earlier in the season.

Everyone loved to be able to predict the first snowfall, and it didn't matter whether there were only a few visible flakes or a foot of snow deposited overnight. The point was, your prediction came true, and with it a certain begrudging admiration of all those to whom you made your prognostication.

With this same élan, we began thinking about next year's garden, forecasting in our minds heavily laden plants, drooping with chiles, beans, tomatoes, and whatever our dreams of abundance brought forth.

One of our abundance dreams was fairly well-fulfilled that year with a great crop of Habanero chile peppers, bright orange. They permeated the kitchen with their unique fragrance, spread out and drying on the wood cook stove that had yet to be used, eager for its first fire. Our other wood stove, used for heating, was lit for the first time when that morning's low was fifteen degrees.

Outside, firewood was stacked in ricks. Each row contained one-third of a chord and formed a large block of wood easily covered with a tarp for the winter.

The carrots were dug, dried, cleaned, and put away in a cooler in the basement. Onions and garlic filled large bowls in the kitchen. Butternut squash were lined up on a rack in the kitchen awaiting the knife to expose their golden flesh: for us these have proven to be the best winter keeper. They also have the most edible meat, with only a small pocket of seeds in one end.

As the world fights to maintain physical boundaries, we can de-construct boundaries by establishing a cybertectonic coterie (from the Latin, *coteré*, meaning *an association of tenant farmers*). At one time, farm communities outnumbered towns and cities. These loosely grouped families had similar concerns and lived, no matter how hard they may have tried to prepare, with the preponderance of chance. There were certain events that could not be foreseen, like early frosts, drought, floods, and infestations, to name a few.

Farmers and gardeners do not have the luxury of firm defining boundaries; they change, moving in and out, here and there, shifting with the conditions of life that necessitate twisting and turning with each event until the harvest is in and stored, and only then can they view and assess their efforts against chance.

At the beginning of spring, we each devise a "story reality," within which we will create a plot and action for us to follow throughout the year. In the garden, we try to define the script as best we can, filling in details and describing the trek for our growing year. We put great effort into this story, checking almanacs, weather reports, our own past records, seed catalogues, and anything else we think might help to keep our story as we have written it.

And then there are our "lived stories," within which we have actual experiences, participation, and intersections with the lived stories of others that help to define our mutually meaningful place in the universal story.

Recently at a fellow gardener's house, we inspected their pepper crop that was strung into ristras, red and dried like crinkled fingers hung in the kitchen above the sink and around cabinets. As we "oohed" and "aahed" over the crop, we acknowledged as to how we too had harvested a good crop. And so, we congratulated each other on the fact that we had both grown, despite the preponderance of chance.

THE GARDEN OBELISK

For us the garden had been over for weeks. Although others in the area continued to have greens and some other produce, a week of hard frosts had put down our lettuce, peppers, eggplants, and squash. Still in the ground were carrots, onions, and beets.

With weather in the high eighties during the day, a feeling remained that we should be looking back over our shoulder at how the garden was doing and why we weren't watering.

It was as if there was a crop of memory that needed attention, only to disappear when the garden gate was opened. The yellow onions had been harvested, brought inside, eaten or stored. The red onions seemed to take forever for their tops to fall over and die off, which sealed the ends and allowed a longer storage period.

It was easy to be lulled into a complacency of warmth, forgetting that the last load of wood needed to be stacked and that three standing dead trees still needed to come down, be cut up and racked, ready for winter.

The Chantenay carrots grew even larger with the late warm days adding to their girth. We liked these carrots for keeping over the winter because they contained more moisture and didn't become wibbly like the thinner ones. We cut off all the green part of their tops and put them in a large cooler after letting them dry for a few days, kept the lid ajar and in a cool place throughout the winter, so moisture could escape and prevent rot.

But we knew that, in the not too distant future, the really hard, cold weather would be here and before the ground froze hard we would need to remove and store what was left in the ground, leaving only memories of last year's crop mingling with the also invisible visions of next spring's planting.

When we wandered out to the garden, we again got caught in that in-between world that we knew once existed and would exist again, yet now the only evidence was stems and leaves and other debris that existed like the enigmatic "*Gone to Croatan*" left by the Roanoke colonists.

What we had been left with was the condition of a "deliberate unseen" that grew clearer as we cleaned remnants out of the garden to avoid mold and hiding places for insects.

The Egyptian obelisk had an infinite point at the top, which spread out and downward, ever widening to its base standing on the ground. On the four sides were messages that, when once read by the viewer on the ground, released a consciousness back up to that infinite point to be dispersed into an otherworld cosmos, there seeking an expression that one day would reappear, at the most appropriate moment, back in the reality from whence it began.

Each of the Egyptian hieroglyphs represented an image in its ideal form, producing in the viewer or reader, a combined "text/image complex" much as the Renaissance emblem books were aligned in sequence to procure an edification in the reader.

These groupings worked on multi-levels: the picture with the associated words; the readers then translating the word; and finally, the intent of the collection to form within the consciousness a representation of a chosen, desired awareness.

As winter closed in through the heat, fewer of the veggie-glyphs remained to speak, and soon the garden that was all ababble in spring, would be silent. Those perfect peppers, growing next to and above the lettuce that shared a closeness with carrot tops gently bending over to provide some symbiotic shade, were read by all those who walked by and glancing, absorbed the emblematic green image/text.

Next spring, someone, somewhere, the time and place unknown to us, will form new gardens, with hands seeding a personal translation of the reappearing energy that at its base, insists that we should grow.

Prairie Dog on alert

QUOTIDIAN DREAMS

Frank's earliest unintentional memories were filled with the smells of fresh cut alfalfa, the dungy odors of pigs, cows, and the horses then used to pull wagons and other machinery that were soon to become motorized and replaced.

It was the consistent events that made impressions: the cloud of dust down the road from the truck coming to load a box of eggs, or the can of milk left out at the edge of the front lawn by the turn-in driveway.

There was a trust that was familiarly anonymous. Many transactions took place without words or meeting; periodic trust that was a part of everyday life.

Without conjuring, there were memories of meowing kittens in the hay barn, wet chicken feathers just dipped in scalding water, and the familiar smell of the chamber pot when the lid was lifted after taking it from under the bed late at night when a trip to the outhouse was too inconvenient.

Some impressions hold us and direct us, allowing movement only when that action is in harmony with those buried desires that we usually never even know exist, much less acknowledge. Frank supposed he was fortunate in that these influences were selective. His family lived in Denver, just down from a company parking lot with another even larger one across the street. The Brown Palace Hotel across the street from his father's office where Frank would often visit, was a place where Vicky's family would often have brunch after leaving their apartments in the Windsor Hotel, which was owned by her grandmother. Frank and Vicky's paths would not yet cross.

Frank's father worked for the Veterans Administration, and was able to take off a month every year to visit the family's Missouri farm. To make the most of time, the family would leave at three or four in the morning. Frank and his younger brother were dragged out in their pajamas, tucked into the back of an old Ford that had become a bed by putting two suitcases on the floor between the back seat and the upright of the front seat. They were snuggled in his father's old world war two sleeping bag and its years of musty basement smell, a light blanket, and their heads on pillows.

It was always wondrous for Frank to awake and look out, trying to figure out how far they had gone, and where they were.

As the years passed and the same route was taken each time, waking became a transition into a then more familiar landscape that was recognized by passing landmarks already having been seen four, five, or six times.

But no matter the distance yet to be traveled, the anticipation remained high, fueled by the past year of finding empty city lots full of weeds and then standing or lying in the middle to get away from the world of cars and houses built only feet apart.

It has been said that smell evokes the greatest and most vivid memories. Frank would tear off handfuls of grass from their Denver lawn and let it dry in the sun, and then lie down by the back porch stairs, pile the dried grass into a small haystack and edge over slowly until his nose brought in the aroma, smelling like the new mown hay he experienced briefly each summer.

One autumn, at our local art gallery, there was an art opening/salon in association with the new showing entitled "Dreamscapes." The subject for discussion was dreams. The afternoon's conversation provided a panoplistic list of what dreams were thought to be.

The only consensus was that we all did it, and somewhere, sometime, and somehow, these mental constructs were etched into our lives, either passively or actively. Often the dream state is like a garden that we plant and ask for a return, which we ourselves cannot produce.

Asking for the answer to a problem to be given in a dream is quite similar to planting a seed and asking for a vegetable. Each is beyond our control in its final result. We can help it along with water and nutrients, or pen and paper by bedside, but in the end, we can only marvel over the redness of the radish, or the simplicity of the solution.

A tangled limb once knocked Frank out of the tree he was trimming, leaving him with broken ribs, a collapsed lung, a fractured pelvis, and ruptured spleen. It was during Frank's recovery that Vicky sat straight up in bed one night and said, "I just had a vision of a three concentric circle herb garden!"

Suddenly the modest vegetable garden they already had on San Juan Island, Washington, became an adjunct to this "vision." Daily it worked itself out, eventuating, building upon itself, and inspiring other gardens to be constructed.

A garden does not grow to fruition by simply planting it and then standing back waiting for a result. It is the continuing daily effort that brings forth the fruit. Often, a seed has been planted within us without us even knowing it, thinking about it, or even realizing its growing presence in our lives.

But all the time it had been there, waiting patiently to sprout, and then with our help, spread its story of our connection to nature.

It would seem that, sometimes, even without plans and directions, we can grow.

Red Kuri Squash

A FEELING OF PROPORTION

It felt like the proportions we seemed to encounter most were those of excess; six-thousand dollar shower curtains, or two-thousand dollar wastebaskets made known to us in our casual reading or viewing. Our minds passed it off with a shrug.

More immediate matters were coming to bear: the fall season had approached with its slower pace and with it a re-assessment of the past growing season. We looked back and remembered there was no killing frost in the month of June that year, which gave us a good start into the summer. The good weather promoted a great garden and early sales at the farmers market.

The monsoons finally showed up in September, a month late that year, providing needed moisture, cooler temperatures, and a change from the day-to-day intense sun. September was also without a killing frost, and the gardens flourished, extending the Ramah Farmers Market by weeks.

Old Gallup bricks line the garden beds

One Sunday we gave our final gardening workshop for the year. Fifteen people attended; the weather brisk, but bearable, with only a small shower in the afternoon while we were out viewing the compost piles.

Our guest speaker related stories of how she helped her grandmother in the Zuni "Waffle Gardens," and she mentioned how most of the time the work was performed in, and for, groups.

That fact suddenly seemed to resonate as we sat around a long homemade table we used at the farmers market for displaying our produce. It was covered with a bright, traditional red and white checkered tablecloth.

Here was gathered a group, those of like-interest, to harvest and share ideas, knowledge, and the noonday meal. Each person, at the end of the day felt as a portion of a whole, proper and significant in his or her proportional group relation, and in new personal relationships.

One's worth in life can be measured by its usefulness to others. Each seed planted is a contribution of continuation, maintaining that unbroken thread that has come down through the ages in fewer and fewer hands. Those who see our gardens, eat the fruits, and are inspired to grow, will feel a greater proportion of life than those whose personal excess can never be contained.

Robert Byrne said, "The purpose of life is a life of purpose." Our purpose is to grow.

LAYING LAYERS

When daylight savings time started, it caused us to down step into a lower time gear. The few lingering garden hangers on, those that had persisted through the light frosts seemed to know, as we, of their denouement. The round compost areas urgently beckoned attention now that evening came earlier, the frost harder, and more often. Daylight hours had been cut short, and choices needed to be made.

We had seen the effects of our choices in the past, good and bad. We surveyed the garden as a whole, interconnected and dependent upon the quality of our decisions. Could our lives be any different? Everything we did influenced everything else.

Choice one: except for a few onions, everything needed to be taken out of the garden and composted. Hog wire circles held the first layer of compost—corn stalks, leaves and cobs on the bottom, providing crisscrossed air spaces that would drain well, provide air circulation, and a base that would not compact.

Choice two: we added a layer of fresh green organic matter, chopped and leveled with the sharp edge of a shovel so decay would heat the pile.

Choice three: there was plenty of dry brown material for the next layer, and for the top of the pile. We had cleaned the covered chicken coop run and decided to use the mix of sand/feed/manure to inoculate the pile, adding microbes to it, (a layer from the layers, as it were).

We repeated these layers until the top of the wire was reached to provide the mass needed for even moisture to insure that the pile worked properly. Composting unified the garden's winter status.

This direction had been signaled by the first two compost bins that contained the cleanings, thinnings, and weedings from the start of this year's garden. Eventually the many layers of the four compost piles would become admixed, and broken down into a commonality.

There is a physics in creative choosing, working with mindal measures. When choices are unified, the quality of those choices becomes apparent over time. Good choices, good results, and consistency unify them. What would the eventual commonality of our personal decision layers become?

The choices we made on how to layer the compost was one thing we could do. Natural events would in time, bring a result. Our responsibility was actively to *do something*—after that it was out of our hands, the results coming from the energies in nature.

Time is the criterion by which the conscious self evaluates the circumstances of life, and by which the conceiving intellect measures and evaluates the facts of temporal existence, as well as the compost.

With the compost, we knew there would be viewable results ten to twelve months later. Unfortunately, the results of personal choices and decisions were not always so apparent or speedy. We viewed events that appeared untouchable to us because of time and distance.

For many, there is an exasperation of not having some alternate/analogous area in their lives, like as a garden, or a compost pile, to re-affirm that, with right-method, intent, and desire, good results can be viewed and evaluated. How fortunate we were to have an avenue that reinforced actions with such tangible results.

Laying layers of Truth, Beauty and Goodness can seem futile in the volatile world in which we live. Our choices are like seeds, and we plant them in good faith, knowing the results are up to time and the process of life. Good, or bad, choice comes to fruition, sooner or later.

Our advantage was that we had planted real seeds and we knew they would grow to their proper end: radish seeds became radishes, not apples. The proof was in the radish.

Keep layering good layers and you will grow.

"Drystack" rock wall raised bed

A STRICKEN WORLD

We heard and read daily how everything had changed, that, "it was different now." We had become familiar with change: bright prospects dashed by an early freeze, or hailstones that shredded the garden plants. The changes that came as a result of the destruction of the World Trade Center buildings in New York, though, were on a much grander scale than our personal failures.

Because of the great number of lives lost, there existed a wider sphere of association even in the middle of nowhere at Pine Hill School on the Navajo Reservation in New Mexico. A teacher next door had a sister in New York who was an eyewitness to some of the events.

We had all heard from everyone we knew, and even those we didn't, what their feelings were: shock, unbelief, dismay, anger, pity, outrage, and helplessness. What could we do?

Ideal possibilities can be brought about within small units of human association. Enthusiasm through friendships enhances joys and triumphs, and stimulates the imagination to find even greater and better solutions to life's problems. How would we remember the loss?

Returning time and again to the past can blur and dull a memory, but creating a memory for the future allows us to communicate, share meanings, and promote values of association.

We can use plants to give expression to change, by creating a "Garden of Memory" for someone living: a mother, brother, neighbor, or friend. We also honor the dead when we honor the living.

Rosemary is the herb of remembrance, a fitting first plant, allowing memories of the past to give appreciation for those in our present.

For the two of us, we planted plant peppermint, symbolizing the wisdom we would continue to seek and a higher understanding and meaning from the past. Then we planted oregano, for the joy and happiness we gave to each other. Thyme, planted for its symbol of courage, reminded us to have the courage to pursue the better way, not always the easiest. For gratitude, Vicky's favorite emotion, we planted Canterbury Bells.

We were grateful for each other, and we were grateful for the influences of others. We were grateful that we had friends to share our expressions, and we looked to the future for a brighter harvest, which we would together grow.

PRODUCING POLICY
An open landscape

Many times we find ourselves in bondage to liberty. Self discipline is all too often a loathsome task, made easier in avoidance by the myriad of distractions we are presented and encouraged to participate in: movies, theme parks, sporting events (live and on TV), and shopping.

To promote a personal "correcting," one needs a policy, a definite course of action adopted for the sake of expediency, one being conducive to advantage or interest as opposed to "right."

For instance, within the gardening community, the "right" way to garden can be anything from hydroponics to permaculture. But it is shared interests that promote advancement in skills, a consistency in direction, a capability for success, and the capacity for growth. This interest-driven part of our shared lives allow us to enlarge and illuminate an "open landscape" rather than legislate it.

What grower doesn't have time to share with another the knowledge gained from experience or secondary sources, friends, magazines, or the internet? A common interest will move us forward. It can be progressive only if we surrender "right" to a greater policy (from the Latin, *polity*, meaning *citizenship*).

We attended the wedding one year of two friends. Later we were in the food line, much of it grown by local gardeners, as were all the flowers cheering the tables with vibrant colors, and the bride's bouquet, that later flew overhead to outstretched arms. As we were loading our plates, a neighbor who lived close by commented on how we seemed only to see each other at celebrations, or community gatherings.

We laughed at the momentary timeliness of it. But later on, thinking about it, we began to notice other "celebrations" that many of these same people attended, all of which brought people together. When the food co-op truck arrived, it was fun and encouraging to watch everyone work together getting the food off the truck, and dividing it quickly, efficiently, and joyfully.

The Ramah Farmers Market was well attended and supported throughout the season, saving locals a fifty-mile trip, one way, to the nearest grocery store for produce. It was held in an area under towering shade trees. Amidst the ring of vendors, tables and chairs were set up, encouraging those who came to stay and visit, catching up on personal events and coming community gatherings.

Many came from as far away as Gallup or Zuni and spent the whole morning with a cup of coffee or tea, sampling from a choice of sweets available, while their fresh organic produce, pastries, and craft items were stored in coolers or in the shade.

As we inexorably globalize, new social paradigms can be established. Food is one common interest that can bring about new agreements that effect human policy. Our gardens, finite expressions of infinite ideals, provide emotional, cultural, and personal experiences of connection. And as one world, one family, we can grow.

Greens box prototype

COMMON GOALS
Reproducing a Consistency

We really wondered, as did Rodney King, why can't we "just get along"? We liked the idea that we should get along, united together for a common goal.

As gardeners, we were the suppliers of not only organic food, but ideas: sustainable organic gardening, selling at a farmer's market, teaching others to grow their own food, and of course, honest coin. We had a common goal in these life's actions—to bring better values into the world.

We tried to express these values in the garden, and gardens grew better when they received consistent attention—watering, weeding, and caring.

A caring consistency soon became an effortless activity, a calming "*action-meditation*" spreading to other areas of our daily lives. We were more apt to be on time when we said we would be somewhere. We were more apt to show up, saying we would. We were more apt to be progressive when presented with a problem, or asked a question. We were more adaptable, and were becoming socially fragrant.

Although we will never meet the majority of our readers, we know our goals are in a similar direction, whether it be in South Africa, Central America, New Zealand, India, England, or Ramah, New Mexico.

It is not so much what we give, as what we share, both among ourselves, and with others, that brings value in the contact; a gift without a giver is barren.

In one workshop on basic rockwork, attended by a dozen people, none had ever worked with rock or cement. Our area abounded in sandstone, giving us access to materials that could be used to make raised bed garden walls, retaining walls, pathways, pools, ponds, and all of the other stone projects that availability presented.

The workshop was a truly an inter-national/multi-cultural event—men, women, Swiss, Zuni, Navajo, and whites. We mixed the first wheelbarrow of cement and then, unbidden, others took over and mixed the next batches, eager to see what it was like to make cement, a mystery and dilemma to many.

As we set the corner stone, the activity began. The goal? To continue to build onto a rock wall started in previous workshops around the base of our chicken coop's stucco wall. We kiddingly told them that the area they were building at (the hen house) showed the confidence we had in their abilities.

Two bags of cement later, what could be done, had been done. It could have been chaotic, tension producing, or individually directionalized, but our common goal was to do and learn together. After one person had mixed a batch or two of cement at the sand pile, instinctively someone else took over the task, allowing that person to experience building the rubble and then setting the rock in the front, neatly continuing the flow, the aesthetics, and the direction that they all sensed they were headed toward.

When we ran out of time and cement, we stood back after a brief cleaning to wonder at what such a scurried activity of commonness had produced. What had not been apparent before now leapt out as our "goal effort," showing our direction and willingness to cooperate, and our willingness to just "get along."

We tried to stress that some aspects of rockwork could become incorporated into our daily lives: strength, beauty, and integrity. The wall was solid, beautiful, and presented an unconscious flow from one person's work to another's that showed a motif and interconnectedness, each having built in harmony on the actions of those working before them.

It was not the wall itself, but the consistency of direction and cooperation, which was given to others, insuring that we all would grow.

WINTER

"Good planting design does not follow a formula. At best, it allows you to experiment with nature and through nature to make an original statement. As in all of the arts, the best garden designers take risks. Only by taking risks can you come up with something exciting and original."

James Van Sweden

Hoar frost

OUR SHARE

Each morning the ice had been thicker. One year we plugged in a small stock tank heater that hung over the edge and lay on the bottom of the birdbath to keep the water from freezing. Until then, it had been warm enough by late morning to melt it, but the birds had been landing earlier, looked down seemingly disappointed, and pecked at the ice. The Audubon Society claims that available water (unfrozen) during the winter months attracts more birds than the feed put out.

Early winter was a transition period of harvesting whatever produce was left in the garden about to freeze and die, collecting and saving seeds, and preparing the garden for the winter.

We attended a potluck "seed exchange" organized by a local woman gardener. Everyone arrived with seeds to share. Outside on a large table there were boxes of flower seeds, perennial wildflower seeds, herb seeds, and vegetable seed. Seed was taken by each, according to their needs and desires for new or different varieties. Much of the seed was grown and harvested locally, a definite benefit for our difficult growing conditions.

Inside, food had been prepared. A large pot of beets simmered on the stove, salads were set out, and other dishes made with locally grown vegetables were on the table.

Piñon Jay

Our geography was such that everyone lived back off the main road. Grocery stores were fifty miles away, so growing your own food, sharing at the farmers market, and just getting together to eat kept everyone in touch.

It was at one such gathering that we found our host standing over the stove, deep-frying a variety of his hot peppers. These "poppers" were filled with different cheeses, dipped in an egg and flour batter, and were fried in the hot oil until they were light brown and tender. Our host and his wife were avid gardeners who maintained a large plot used and shared by their extended family.

Probably the most discussed garden plant, and locally the most commonly grown after the tomato, were hot and sweet peppers. Everyone had a favorite, but for an all-around pepper with good flavor and fire, it was hard to beat the Jalapeno. They are dark green, or red when fully ripened, with a firm flesh that makes them great for cooking.

We talked about pepper varieties as we watched them sizzle in the hot canola oil. The demand for them was so great that we began to stuff the peppers in an assembly line fashion. We made poppers until someone finally said, "Enough!"

Carl Jung put forth the concept of a collective unconscious mind that if probed, would reveal some common global strands, which bind us. These strands enter this realm through the everyday passageways from which, unfortunately, most people have become disassociated.

Yet, riding near the surface of this collective is a realization of our interdependence, and if only accessed, could produce a more harmonic world.

But instead, our communication system capabilities transfer the traumas of tsunamis, earthquakes, hurricanes, wars, and suicide bombings, and enter our collective mind with such regularity and intensity that it produces what Immanuel Velikovsky calls a "collective amnesia."

As organisms in a cosmic garden, we have allowed the weeds of suspicion and distrust to grow unchecked as they use up resources and we are denied the nourishment we so desperately need.

One cannot get away from the fact that weeding a whole garden takes time. But it is not in the nature of a gardener to be a pessimist; these destructive weeds can be pulled and used as compost to re-vitalize the garden's replacement crop of Truth, Beauty, and Goodness.

From these harvests will come a new *Weltanschauung*: a comprehensive conception or image of civilization, of the universe, and man's relation to it.

It is only by harvesting and sharing the good that we will grow.

POPPING AS CORN

We enjoyed popped corn. It came in all colors—red, blue, white, yellow, pink, calico, and deep red. Varieties included strawberry shaped, Japanese hull less, and an extra early heirloom dwarf, Tom Thumb.

Because we ate so much we had a lot of experience cooking it. We say cooked instead of popped because cook means to prepare by the "action of heat," and by the action of heat (cooking) we were able to initiate rapid transformations.

Corn pops because of the moisture stored in its kernels. We kept our un-popped corn in a quart mason jar in the back of the refrigerator. After removing it from the store bag, we wet the inside of the jar before adding the kernels, and then shook the jar. Adding moisture was what made them pop so well.

We saw cooking corn as the end of a gardening effort, turning hard un-chewable kernels into light, soft morsels. We liked to use a deep, heavy steel pot with a tight lid. We poured organic high-heat sunflower oil in the bottom, a thin layer, enough that each kernel got a good coating. We measured a few kernels more than a one-half cup.

We had a gas stove so we turned the burner on high, placed the pot on it, and didn't move it. This got all the kernels evenly hot on the bottom. It was enjoyable to hear that first kernel bursting, followed closely by more and then more.

When the popping became regular, we slipped on oven mitts and grabbed the handle sides, lifting the pot slightly off the flame. Once the popping increased, we lifted it a bit higher and adjusted the height to find just the right temperature.

It was then that popping corn was such a pleasure, with the smell, the sounds of bursting kernels hitting the lid, and working the pot over the open flame, cooking them until they all burst open to perfection. Searching the bottom bits of one batch we made, we found only two un-popped kernels.

When we were sure that no more would pop, we took off the lid and poured the popped corn into a large, flowered enamel pan we bought when there was a country store at Pine Hill. Then we dribbled some melted organic butter over the popcorn, and salted it lightly.

We were constantly made aware of the popularity of microwave popcorn, and we must admit, that when someone cooked a bag of it, it smelled good, and it was fast to prepare, but for us, it was not as good, nor as rewarding, as when cooked the old fashioned way.

The approach of spring will foreshadow signs that "the action of heat" would bring the popping open of seeds and warming the soil for tiny feeder roots to seek and gather nutrients. If the soil was cold, it closed the feeding system at the bottom of their roots and there was slower growth. Heat also increased microbial activity in the soil, releasing nutrients for the little seedlings first meals

As the temperatures increased, seeds seem to "pop" out of the ground, first a few, and then more, until the beds were filled, growth was rapid, and harvest could begin.

For many, life is a flinty, hard existence that cannot be opened, transformed, or used to its fullest potential. We are in many ways, the action of heat. It was in the warm shallows of ancient waters that the first slow popping of life began, and then with more and more of this bursting life, it grew to what we are today.

Once we find our action-of-heat-level, we will become someone useful, nutritional, and palatable for the universe, and with a pop, we can grow.

Early morning after a heavy snowfall

A LINGERING GLOW

Aside from dropping temperatures, heavier clothing, and a change to daylight savings time, the distant whine of a neighbor's chain saw cutting firewood announced that preparation would soon be needed for winter.

By late morning, if the sky was clear, the sun was warm and if there was no breeze, you could take off your coat. Soon, the birdbath would need a heater to keep it from freezing solid.

Last year we used less than two chords of firewood to heat our house for the winter. Some days we started a fire in the morning and then depending upon how cold it was, we either kept it going until bedtime, or would let it go out early in the day. In the deep of winter's cold, we kept the fire going all night by adding a large round of juniper, which would leave enough coals in the morning to start the morning fire.

But, now was the time to get rid of the small pieces of odds and ends from last year's wood pile, and to cleanup scraps from all the summer projects that left short pieces of lumber lying around—pieces that would give heat and burn fairly fast, not the round all-nighters that would be needed in January and February.

We had a wood cook stove in the kitchen that took the shorter wood and the smaller tree limbs. Crumpled paper and kindling were kept "ready to light" for the mornings when the temperature had dropped overnight and we wanted to quickly take the chill off the kitchen, get the stove hot, and cook sourdough pancakes and eggs on top of its well-seasoned surface.

The main wood supply was from One-seed juniper (Juniperus monosperma), although Rocky Mountain juniper (Juniperus scopulorum) and Alligator juniper (Juniperus deppeana) grew in this area. The other main wood source was piñon pine (Pinus edulis) which we gathered from dead branches or from cutting standing dead trees.

The wood we used the least was Ponderosa pine (Pinus ponderosa) since it did not give off as much heat as juniper or piñon. One year, a freak windstorm blew down one of our older ponderosa and gave us at least a chord of wood.

The trees in our area are very slow growing, not like the fast growing Alder and Fir we were able to grow in a wood-lot fashion on San Juan Island in Washington State, so we were judicious from which trees we would harvest, wood that had fallen naturally or blown down, and which had stayed off the ground for years.

We hauled wood in from the main pile and stacked it on the covered porch for easy access. It was divided into sections, from the smallest to the largest, kindling, medium size for day fires and the cook stove, and the larger overnight pieces.

Wood fires give off a deeper, warming heat, appreciated more when coming in from the cold. The scent of piñon pine evoked a connection to those who lived here in the past who must have felt the same appreciation as we do for the wood they gathered and burned from the same species. The sun had been the main provider of warmth during the busy season. In winter, a fire contained in a hearth allowed comfort, time for reflection, and inner growth.

We were fortunate to live in a rural area that still had wood for harvest that could be salvaged without changing or destroying the ecology.

In the evenings, watching the lingering coals, we had the feeling we would grow.

THANKS-GIVING
A Natural Service

At this time of year, our garden was dormant, yet still contained lettuce, kale, chard, beets, carrots, onions, and parsnips, as we anticipated the approaching final killing freeze with its cold plunge into the winter months. Yet, the world outside the garden daily erupted, regardless of the season with ever widening divisive wedges that broadened our separation; those less obvious than distance, language, religion, and culture.

And so we headed toward that day known as Thanksgiving, a day when millions of hearts, minds, and lips would be grateful for what they felt they had received of divine bounty, the "thanks" often overriding the "giving." Lip service for the day's comforts, along with extended-meal-memories as entrées, lulled anxiety for the moment, and provided the feeling of "duty done."

We all search for a "doable." A garden allows for advancement of a world culture as we participate, express, and live it. Instead of this exercise broadening chasms, the garden allows a felt presence of immediate experience, connecting us to an archaic past of authentic commonness.

Marshall McLuhan believed that the planetary human culture, the "global village," would be "tribal" in character. In biology, a tribe is the classification of plants and animals. "Whole" systems depend on co-adaptive evolution and symbiotic relationships, cooperative strategies that benefit the entire system.

Plants have the ability to maximize cooperation with other plant species as they interact with each other through the tangled mat of roots that connect them all to the sources of their nutrition, and to each other. In society, the mat of roots that connects us all should be providing a base for intellectual peace, moral satisfaction, spiritual joy, social progress, and cosmic wisdom.

Plants preceded animals in evolution. What is needed now is to use technology to rediscover and adopt the ways of that "matrix of vegetable intelligence" to advance human culture.

Thanks-Giving combines gratitude and service. Gratitude, (from the Latin, *gratis*, meaning *pleasing*), and service (from the Latin, *Serv*, meaning *someone who does "what needs to be done"*). What it is it that we can do that is pleasing and needs to be done? We can grow.

SEASONINGS

Thanksgiving brought the snow mentioned as "traditional" in most of our neighbors' pasts, as told around the food-laden table in the early afternoon as we anticipated the later arrival of the others in our small community for the dessert feast.

The low temperature of the night was twelve below zero. 'Tis the season indeed: Thanksgiving, winter, Christmas, and the New Year.

Season is from the Latin, *sation*, meaning *a sowing*, or *a sowing time*. But what do we sow in these conditions? Since we could not plant any seeds in our frozen garden outside, the season's sowing must be made for the garden within. In the spring, we selected the seeds and plants that were nurtured until summer's end. The garden was usually a success, because much of it had been made ready beforehand by a readiness of "experience preparation." We knew how to handle the tiller, harden off the transplants, and perform the many other skills needed to go from seed to fruition.

The garden within is not seeded by us. Instead, we are planted with the seeds of possibility, scattered on us like salt. We are planted to bring forth Truth as we live daily in the material world, working with the universal energies that are available to us all. We are planted to bring forth Beauty as we use our minds to decide and choose the higher and better way of dealing with material events. We are planted to bring forth Goodness, by allowing our spirit nature to guide us in our dealings with each other.

To be in readiness for the seeding of our garden within, we need to ask: Have we prepared the soil for their acceptance? Have we acquired the nutrients for them to grow? Is our dedication to keeping the weeds out, strong? Do we have that water of life that would grow them to fruition?

One night, with the wind blowing and the temperature low, one of our nine cats wanted to go out the back door. He stood patiently waiting for the crack to open so he could slip through. We pulled back the door and he took two quick steps forward, felt the cold wind, and backed away.

We shut the door thinking, "smart cat." A few minutes later he was at the door again, so being the obliging type, we opened it again. This time he was ready, steeled against the elements and determined to brave whatever there was. Without hesitation, he slipped into the cold night air.

Sometimes we just have to know what we are facing to take those forward steps so we can grow.

House Finches searching for food

TRANSITION
A light behind the hill

The garden was asleep for the winter, nestled under a brown alfalfa blanket of mulch, and nutrients added earlier with tilling would be dispersed and absorbed into the de-compacted soil.

From the entrance at the garden gate, the garden view was a flat-sameness resembling an awaiting canvas. Checking the compost piles and the worm beds, we found the wigglers had gone deeper into the pile with the lowering temperatures.

Our woodpile had been covered with a tarp to protect it from the inevitable rain and snow. The strawbale wall had on its stucco color coat, waterproofing and protecting it from winter weather.

In the late afternoon, the sun seemed all too anxious to disappear behind the west horizon, leaving only moments to work on lingering projects and do the daily chores. Cold and dark forced us to enter into the house, leaving the woodpile, the garden, and the worms.

The end of another year approached, the holiday season a denouement of the year's events. It felt good to close the sometime stressful, mostly busy, always exciting year. Just as the turning of the calendar page finalized our year's endeavors with mindal revisions, so did it also allow our imaginations to leap with prospects and ideas for the coming year.

At this time of year our world was lit by the morning sun, not coming over the horizon to full light but showing as lengthened rays, shooting between the canyons cut deep by ancient waters. It was a morning hint, a gist of what would be increased as the day progressed. Soon, it too would be leaving its winter den to help us splash diversity on the now blank garden canvas.

Once again we approached the world with new ideas for gardens, each of us creating a matrix that contained our beliefs and desires. The garden was an entry point of commonality that provided us with the felt presence of immediate experience. With this experience, we could touch and help awaken all those who may have felt isolated, distanced, and alone on this planet.

The Navajo have a saying that, "You can't wake a person who is pretending to be asleep." This Snow-White-like-poison-apple (technology, economics, injustice, violence, or the rush of life many may have bitten) had caused a trance-like condition of feeling helpless, and of not being able to relate to, or help, others.

It is true that we, in and of ourselves, could not wake them: but a garden could reconnect with forces and energies that were able to reopen eyes and awaken them to the inextricable relationship they had to each person on this conceptually shrinking planet.

We looked forward to spring when the sun would rise above the hill, show forth its full light, and aid us in bringing forth the two greatest crops we could grow—peace and goodwill.

PROVING GROUNDS

We grow under the auspice of laws that have been enjoined with the progression of our minds to more fully relate to our place in the universe.

A fair amount of science is needed in the garden—an understanding of pH values, chemical reactive fertilizers, meteorology, and general physics. We use empirical methods to ascertain weather outcomes—such as looking up and seeing the wispy wind-blown clouds known as "horse's manes" high in the sky and knowing that a change is coming, but not knowing the extent or direction of that change.

We build on where we start, and start with what we know, and what we know was taught, either by others, or ourselves. Science in agriculture has given us cloning, hydroponics, and genetic engineering. When we adopt a plant, we adopt the science behind it.

Snow receeding from the "trinket garden"

When we buy a Poinsettia for Christmas, most fail to realize it is probably descended from a cutting (a clone) of a plant discovered in Mexico in 1828. From 1923 until the early 1960s, all of the principal cultivars of commercial importance were clones from an original "Oak Leaf" seedling.

Hydroponics, using liquid nutrients, demonstrates that our soil is simply a holding agent.

Genetic engineering allows insights into the hard-wired nucleus containing the genetic keys for change and adaptation to numerous environmental conditions, but just as the with horse's manes, what the change will bring is dependent upon unknown forces.

Then there is the age old question of "nature or nurture?" Our gardens give us a good answer: no matter how vibrant the seed may be initially, if it is not nurtured it will only be able to fulfill a small portion of its locked-in destiny potential.

The name protein is from the Greek, *Proteios,* meaning, *primary element.* Proteins are the primary components of all plant and animal cells. Each protein has its own unique sculpture, referred to as its "conformation, providing the organism its structure and formation."

Until recently, science has proceeded down a path apparent, one that James Watson and Francis Crick began, and has since developed into the "Primacy of DNA." This primacy concludes that DNA controls and determines the character of an organism.

However, studies by Dr. Bruce Lipton, a research scientist at Stanford University show that genes are regulated by "environmental signals." Cells can read the environment and their protein receptors respond to vibrational frequencies through a process known as "electroconformation coupling." These receptors convert awareness of the environment into "physical sensations" providing perceptions of reality.

But, because we are often consciously unaware of what happens around us, or we misinterpret it, it becomes necessary that our beliefs should control our perspectives.

These environmental vibrations are received and translated through cell membranes. These membranes are able to perform this function because, based upon the organization of its phospholipid molecules, the membrane acts as a crystal, and information crosses the hydropholaic barrier rendering the membrane a semiconductor, endowing it with proteins that function as gates (receptors) and channels. As a liquid crystal semiconductor with gates and channels, this membrane becomes an information processing transistor, or an organic computer chip.

Science, once establishing its "facts," continues to support only its own perspectives—even in the face of experiments that show plants can benefit from electricity, electromagnetism, music, or good thoughts.

Until Rachel Carlson demonstrated the interconnectedness of our environmental actions, DDT was used and over used as a matter of routine as a pesticide. The shift towards the idea of a more organic, earth-friendly environmental growing of our foods has been slow, and for many, seen as an impossible goal to achieve.

Such thoughts and expressed views are the vibrations that most people are subject to, and hence the result of a perspective of limitation and misdirection. It is then imperative that our beliefs become the designing force toward our garden within as well as the garden outside.

Just as we look to the next season for newness, so must we look to new thinking and new ideas, discarding the scaffolding that has brought us this far, but has now become an obstacle for new growth.

Our next steps will be of experimentation and trial, new thinking and discovering for others and ourselves, a better direction in which we can grow.

VADE MACUM

The temperature had suddenly dropped below zero degrees F. at night, and the only things growing outside were people's woodpiles. Our tomato plant in the greenhouse finally froze, its leaves hanging like green tinsel on a Christmas tree.

The snow that always seemed to come on Thanksgiving had waited a couple of days and blew in late at night, surprising all those who went to bed early with a high-wind, drift-sculptured landscape in the morning.

Most people in our area who had immediate family members living nearby were descendents of those who first arrived and stayed.

Those early Mormon settlers, chased out of their community in Mexico, arrived here at the beginning of winter, and chose it as a place to stop, raise their families, and re-establish their community, which was eventually named Ramah.

Probably the one thing most associated with these settlers was their emphasis on family. The original families' names crop up on street signs, high mesas, and a cattle company.

Wood stoves were the main heat source in many homes, and during winter with the temperatures dropping, it didn't take more than a day of not having a fire to have a house freeze, pipes burst, and houseplants die.

Livestock needed the ice in their tanks broken, and to be fed their daily ration of hay. Pets needed extra food and water to counteract the blowing cold. Holidays, especially in winter, were not a time for travel.

But, holidays were a great time for locals to gather and thank each other for the support and helping hands given throughout the year. That year we only had to travel a quarter- mile to reach our gathering place for Thanksgiving.

We took pecan pie and potatoes mashed with sour cream, garlic, and jalapenos. There were two turkeys and numerous other dishes, all cooked with loving care, as tasting verified.

The large living room was just able to hold the thirty or so people who circled, joined hands, and stood reflecting silently on their good fortune to be present. Two standing next to each other kissed, and a voice cried, "Pass it on!" and so around it went, left and right, ending back with the original two.

The laughter and joy soon became hunger and someone said, "Let's eat." Everyone dropped hands and headed for the kitchen, still in line as it wound around the food and back out to where each chose a place to sit. Some sat on the stone hearth, feeling the fire while others sat and looked out at the Zuni Mountains from the living room. A few sat at the dining room table near the food. We sat at a round table in a large sunroom, warm amongst tall plants.

Later in the evening, sitting by the fire, guitars were passed around. Songs of many genres were sung, some prompting a sing along, others just for quiet listening. Stories were told, and laughter echoed into the darkness.

During the evening, we were approached by a friend and gardener, who hoped to fill our space at the farmers market, and asked us if we had any suggestions. This was wonderful news for us, and for the community. During the next hour, we explained some of what we had learned from our years of gardening, servicing restaurants, selling directly from the gardens and participating in farmers markets. He mentioned that he had brought the salad, grown in his cold frame, and was pleased that we had identified the little leaves of Tat Soi.

Gardeners, after years of experience, become a walking "*vade mecum*," a ready reference of information useful to others. Our method of "small crops and high rotation" fit right in with his proposed approach. We were pleased to be able to give valuable information that would help to continue a work that we had done for years.

Most in attendance were not usually seen at other community affairs. Someone commented how they were all a community "underground." But, underground is where roots are, where fruits get nourishment, and that place which provides stability for growth potential.

Looking around at those who were present we became aware of a dedication to simple living, organic foods, like-mindedness, and a desire to make the world a better place through effort. Effort does not always produce joy, but there is no happiness without intelligent effort.

We were thankful we lived in an area promoting the values of brotherhood, sisterhood, cooperation, and a unity of spirit and insight, providing the soil from which we all could grow.

UNDER THE COVER OF EVENTS
Down the Road

Visitors during winter months, when asking to see the garden, had to be satisfied with a walk down a snow-shoveled trail to view the gardens, using more imagination than sight, as we talked about the crops and methods that would come about at a later time. In some ways this was a good thing.

One visitor from Minnesota had become a vegetarian a few years ago, and his garden was taking on a new importance in his life. By projecting information into the future, we were able to by-pass the immediacy of the drifting snow.

It is at this time of year that we find ourselves in a back-to-back situation: the media provided us memories of the past year's events and pushed us into a new calendar year of resolutions and wonderings. The winds of past events, so important and earth changing, now barely rippled the surface of our lives, leaving what lay underneath to provide the appropriate tack to safe harbor.

Julian Jaynes said that, "History does not move by leaps into unrelated novelty, but rather by the selective emphasis of aspects of its own immediate past." But all too often it is the "leaps into unrelated novelty" from which we are asked to shape our world; the aspects of our "immediate past" covered by "snow" only reveal the outlines of future promise.

These outlines that were now submerged were the true and powerful currents that flowed beneath the news/events/announcements, running deep into an archaic past of common connection. This thread now ran from Minnesota to New Mexico as a sign post of direction: regardless of what was seen on the surface, our inner vision traveled the same trail.

The drumming had already started by the time we arrived at a neighborhood gathering. The large living room was ringed with people pounding out rhythms, accompanied by others on wooden sticks, tambourines, a cow bell, and all manner of other instruments shaken, tapped, and scratched.

Some danced free style in the middle of the room, each giving expression to their individual mood, style, and feeling of the moment. Food and drink in the kitchen provided a second gathering area.

There we met gardeners from Taos, New Mexico and San Francisco, California, as we shared experiences, methods, and the thrust or direction of their gardens. All agreed that the "people connection" was the end goal, although each of us was taking a divergent route.

Outside, in a nearby field, an old barn built in the forties with discarded wooden ammunition crates from Fort Wingate had fallen down, been pushed into a pile, and was to be lit afire and watched late into the evening.

This gathering interwove many a stream of our ancient past into a flowing direction of purpose and continuity, showing once again the outlines of our human destiny, now covered with a soon to melt obscurity. Thus, our visions of spring, looked forward to, worked toward, and shared, would provide the soil in which, together, we could grow.

The silence of winter

GETTING IN LINE

It was always surprising when December twenty-second arrived and suddenly winter was declared to be "official." Considering the fact our low had already been a minus fourteen degrees F. and the ground had been white with snow for weeks that year, having the "arrival" of winter announced seemed anti-climatic. Dog and chicken water, ponds, and the birdbath had needed heaters to keep them free of ice.

Our chores spoke of a different season. The kindling box needed to be refilled with split cedar, the appropriate size wood needed to be put on the porch for the woodstove and cookstove. Instead of tilling the garden beds, watering and weeding, splitting wood and shoveling snow was the order of the day. When we went to town, the decorations, the music, and the greater number of shoppers told us more about a holiday than a "declared" season.

We knew it was winter when we could no longer just run out the door. Now we needed to sit down, put on waterproof boots, don vests, down jackets, gloves, hats, and scarves. The bird feeder seemed empty all the time. With the cold and lower sun, the chickens gave us fewer eggs. The pet food bowls needed filling more often.

We drove down our driveway using four-wheel drive to get to the paved road. The weather channel was checked more often to see when the next system was coming in, and what we needed to do before it arrived. The smell of hot chocolate filled the kitchen. Sourdough pancakes were made on top of the wood cookstove.

Taking our dogs for walks provided laughter as they ran scooping snow into their mouths, jumping and running as they tossed the dry powder glistening into the air.

Little prints in the snow reminded us of how many rabbits and other smaller creatures there were. Every once in a while, the abrupt stop of prints ended by the pattern of owl wings in the snow.

But, the surest sign of winter, which all gardeners shared, was the sudden appearance of seed catalogs in the mail. We had received an *R. H. Shumway Seedsman* catalog, advertising their "*Good Seed Cheap,*" and "*A Business Built on Fairness, Honesty and Good Service.*" At ten by thirteen inches, it was the largest catalog we received.

Seeds of Change and *Johnny's Selected Seeds,* with their high quality photos on glossy paper, gave each example a grower's desired perfection. They all had something new to try; an improved variety, a recently found heritage seed, or a newly developed early bloomer. We seemed always to think about trying one of each, even though most were not suited for our climate.

Experience reminded us of what happened the first time we tried to grow one-hundred-twenty day melons in our ninety-day or less New Mexico high desert growing season. But sometimes it worked, with protective cloches, mulch, early starting of seeds and late transplanting, and all the other tricks we had learned over the years.

New varieties do not appear suddenly, they are bred by isolating desired qualities until the breeder was satisfied with the results of his harvest. The gardener harvests more than what is given by a plant; the gardener plants part of himself along with the radish, lettuce, and carrot seed; others then can benefit from that planting.

The old standbys provided us with reliability, yet it was the combining of new and better traits that gave us progress, the watchword of the universe. As moves the part, so moves the whole. How could we become a new variety?

Just as we mulched, cloched, and provided care for plants that needed our assistance, we helped ourselves by nurturing tolerance, understanding, patience, loyalty, honesty, gentleness, peace, love, and our faith in goodness.

By encouraging these desired qualities in ourselves, we can become a better variety, moment by moment, adding these desirable traits until we become satisfied with the results of the harvest we have grown.

FILLING THE RICTUS

One night we were invited to a neighborhood winter solstice gathering/pot-luck. A table was filled with a platter of turkey, dressing, salads, and a variety of other foods.

Later, after everyone had eaten, we gathered outside in the dark under the vast, starry, New Mexico sky, and stood around a rock fire pit filled with sticks, each first having been lit in the hearth of each household represented, and then added to the pile to be re-kindled. Our hostess lit the paper underneath, giving life to the soon to be blazing fire.

There were chairs and benches around the perimeter; others choose to stand. Our hostess then spoke of community, commitment, and the commonality symbolized by the burning sticks each had brought for starting the community fire.

A round of drumming and singing followed, with several of the braver ones gleefully jumping over the burning fire. It was also the birthday of one of our neighbors, so we sang "Happy Birthday," and then broke into a rousing "For He's a Jolly Good Fellow."

Looking around the fire circle, it was evident that many lifestyles were present. In the bathroom, there was a book of photographs depicting the flavor of the nineteen-sixties. The photos captured a spirit and energy that many of us that evening remembered well.

Later, as the embers dimmed, we said our "Good Nights," and drove home down the snowy two-tire-track back road. After a foot of snow had fallen, one of our neighbors had plowed the road using a "V" shaped I-beam from an old house trailer.

Progress needs enthusiasm. No project can get finished without a goal, determination, and the desire to make it all happen. One is easily propelled in the spring when the days are pleasant and warm, the newness of activity is novel, and a vision of what is to be is stimulated.

It was only late in the gardening season, when, day after day, one had nurtured, urged, and tried to provide a consistent environment for plant growth, that a certain weariness began to set in. The garden provided us with foods to nourish our bodies, but sustenance for the spirit could only come from others in spirit.

Those winter days, with sub-zero temperatures and snow that would remain on the north facing slopes until spring, seemed to represent a condition of spirit felt throughout the world.

While many can find food for the body, few can find food to nurture the spirit, allowing it to be productive. And it will only be by spirit recognition that the world will be able to bring about group understanding, mutual appreciation, fraternal fellowship, spiritual communion, and divine harmony.

All over this nest of a world, people, like baby robins, stretch upward with an open rictus, desiring a parent's feeding.

It is an opportunity incumbent upon us to feed each hungry mouth as we pass by—with a smile, a nod of recognition, or a kind word—fruits that are plentiful, even in this frozen season. It is only when others have been fed that we can grow.

"Piñoncicles"

A CONVINCING SELF

The end of the year loomed suddenly, reminding us of all those unfinished projects, projects not yet started, and a few projects finished. For us that year, undertakings had ranged from gardening, building a formal tea garden, giving workshops, and starting a new home on the west edge of our fifty-four acres. We began the project in spring, and had no idea when it would be completed, nor when we would be able to move. It had been closed-in for the winter, which allowed us to keep working on the inside.

There are two types of Navajo hogans, male and female. The door always opens to the east greeting the rising sun, welcoming beauty and goodness at the beginning of each day. We were building an eight-sided female hogan, which was the larger traditional living and nurturing area. The smaller cone-shaped male hogan was the place for healing rituals and purifying ceremonial fires.

Because we were building a new home, we did not plant a large garden that year, only a small one for our own sustenance, so we did not sell produce at the farmers market. We used our accrued skills to give workshops, write more gardening articles, and discovered new ways to pass along garden related information.

With most other projects finished, we looked forward to new goals that would hopefully provide the opportunity to become more convincing (from the Latin, *convince*, meaning *to prove right or wrong, true or false*).

The gardens had given us the time and methods to work on ourselves while we worked with and for others. Taking care of plants had put us on a path of consistency—watering, weeding, and watching.

The farmers market had given us a dedication to those who came each week, looking forward to fresh organic vegetables and some "local" conversation. Our workshops had given us unity with others of like mind.

A completion of the large scale gardening phase of our lives provided us with a wistful satisfaction, seen through a progression of over thirty growing seasons.

We have enjoyed, and will continue to enjoy, working with and using the natural energies of the universe—water, sun, and the earth. We have endeavored to make gardens beautiful, and we have been fortunate to have been able to spiritually sup with so many people.

Marshall McLuhan said, "The affairs of the world are now dependent upon the highest information of which man is capable. The word information means pattern, not raw data."

Capabilities are only achieved through effort. If our efforts in the garden are to bring about Truth, Beauty, and Goodness, then the patterns of consistency, dedication, and spiritual unity will grow a convincing self.

Growth is the information of unity direction that we can grow.

GROWING THROUGH PERIMETERS

January first approached like an abrupt closing of the garden gate. Looking back on the year we could see certain boundaries that became expanded: the cat side of the family grew when two shelter kittens came our way, and a few months later a mother cat, starving and in need of a home, pushed the perimeter out to a total of ten.

Then, while feeding a neighbor's cat, a small black and white skinny puppy appeared out of nowhere, and jumped into our arms. We took her home, fed her, and watched as she peacefully fell asleep by the woodstove. She had been sustaining herself on stinkbugs—as was evidenced the next day when she relieved herself in the yard. Now the dog perimeter had been pushed out to three.

More people have moved into the area and many stopped by the farmer's market this summer, expanding those perimeters.

Some came to our workshops, and others came out to visit the gardens to get ideas for their own soon-to-be-started gardens. Food is a wonderfully compatible common denominator for growing wider the perimeters of human association. Almost every day someone new had signed up for our online newsletter from faraway places like South Africa, Bangladesh, Australia, New Zealand, the Philippines, and Portugal, to name a few, each person reading and expanding by the association.

Corral fences and garden fences, the boards, bricks, and rocks used for raised beds, were physical perimeters that were moved and built. Other perimeters were spiritual—changed only by our personal growth.

Events throughout the year expanded our perimeters of compassion, sympathy, and understanding. Nurtured by television, the internet, and discussions with everyone met, the boundaries of our spiritual gardens within expanded. Values, and priorities, changed, our new crop of understanding others grew rapidly, but harvesting was slowed by internal questions of ethics, morals, and duties.

Picking unripe fruit benefits no one.

Boundaries are necessary steps in personal growth. They are the foundation for understanding and interpreting one's self-reality. These new foundations become the next inner-garden perimeters to be expanded, an ever-widening arena for growth.

Having closed the garden gate, we could view the physical and personal work that had been done, remember and evaluate those seeds which had been planted and grew, and we looked forward to new endeavors.

These moments of perspective, when seen from behind the garden gate, can be defining moments for creativity and self-reality. We amend our inner-gardens with resolve, just as we add compost to our garden outside, to nurture our next year's crop. From these gardens, we will grow the real fruits of our labors, spiritual and physical.

Across the valley on a snowy winter's day

ERGODIC REMEMBRANCE

Valentine's Day was special for us. We gave each other simple things. For Vicky, a small pair of stud earrings made by a Navajo woman who sold at the school during the holiday season. For Frank, a new pair of seventy-two inch leather boot laces.

Giving is an interesting thing. Certainly, generosity prompts the desire to bestow a gift upon another. And it is true that it is better to give than to receive. But what do we give? It appears easy to find "things" since the media provides us with examples of every imaginable gift. Catalogues explore the realm from the ridiculously expensive to the sensibly cheap.

Some people had been raised with financial expression as a means of communicating their closeness. This tendency and method of gifting was somewhat surprising, since hunger and famine still existed alongside reams of catalogues, high-end stores, and shopping malls.

About this time each year, we would go into our greenhouse and clone three different species of rosemary, a traditional symbol of remembrance. We filled seedling trays (each hole about one inch across, and one and one half inch deep) with organic potting soil, set each in its tray of warm water, and began to take cuttings.

Each cutting was about four inches long, or the width of one's hand, (the linear measure used to determine the height of a horse) and had proven to be a convenient and consistent method of measure for making clones.

After cutting the stem on a diagonal (so it wouldn't sit flat on the bottom of the pot and cut off the oxygen and water supply) we removed one third of the bottom leaves, dipped the stem in Rootone, and placed it into the soil until it touched the very bottom of the tray. We had already pre-soaked the soil to stop the stems from drying up and preventing rooting.

The heating mat helped promote rooting by keeping the temperature constant, around eighty degrees F. We left the cuttings in these trays for about three weeks, and when they started to send little roots out of the bottom, we transplanted them into four inch pots, and fed them Alaska fish emulsion that gave them a quick spurt of growth.

Using this method, we were able to reproduce and continue the three strains, each having their own unique smell, color, and shape.

The heating mat also warmed the soil for newly planted seeds, artichokes, onions, hardy perennial flowers, and culinary herbs. With the increasing pull of the moon into its second quarter, the seeds had already started to leap out of the planting mix, stretching their new shoots into the warmth of the sunlight.

Genetic engineering is a process of artificially modifying plant (and animal) cells by cutting and splicing DNA in order to transfer supposed desirable qualities (pesticide or insect resistance). However, the proteins in transferred genes may develop unexpected reactions or have potentially toxic effects that would be passed on to subsequent generations, ultimately affecting our ability to maintain any consistency in seeds or crops.

For all the suspected and predicted problems that genetic modification (GM) may bring about (inter-specie mutation, super weeds, food allergies, health problems), the one factor that is indisputable is loss of genetic diversity.

The importance of biodiversity includes socio-cultural, economic, and environmental elements. Genetic biodiversity provides not only healthy crops, it also allows for new plant and seed varieties, helping to maintain soil microorganisms and fertility.

A constancy of traits is desirable—once gardeners find the "right" tomato, they tend to grow that variety for years, save their own seeds, and perpetuate their own crops. What they have then produced is an ergodic population, one in which any single tomato is representative of the entire crop. Heritage seed is consistent for generations.

Our crop of cloned Rosemary is ergodic, the salient characteristics of each new clone are essentially identical with the mother plant.

As we hold onto our genetic diversity as individuals, let us also strive to produce an ergodic population by encouraging the qualities of kindness, sharing, giving, and generosity. Let us also promote a desire to spread these traits and grow an ergodic community, town, state, country, and world.

We have the inherent ability to clone our good qualities, pass them on, and prove that we can grow.

HEURISTIC NAIVETÉ

As snow storms blew in, the ground increasingly whitened, adding needed moisture for all the spring sprouting seeds just beneath the surface, waiting for the right conditions to emerge and provide fresh tender shoots for small scurrying animals like the kangaroo rat and the numerous prairie dogs. The vegetation would add nutrients to the soil once their days in the sun were over.

They would also provide a welcome splash of color for us to enjoy and be inspired by as we too were plied with new growth and inspiration. What snow fell and remained would disappear rapidly into the ground, the climbing sun not allowing a sustained cold to remain.

The greenhouse was filling up. The first planted seed trays had sprouted. Small plants transferred into four-inch pots would be moved to the greenhouse out by the garden to be hardened off and once well rooted, transplanted into the ground where there would be immediate new root growth into the surrounding soil.

We had started the second set of seed trays that would provide, down the line, backups (in case of a late frost) and a supply of plants for continuous growing: harvest one, pop in another, without having to wait for germination and growth.

At a potluck, we met a man from Vermont who was an organic gardener. We didn't get a chance to talk too much amid the swirl of conversations taking place about world events, some hawks, some doves, each flapping their wings, fanning a spark of personal idealism. At times, like-minded groups gravitated together solidifying their ideas with more hushed voices than had been used with their opposition.

A few days later, the fellow gardener came for a visit. We talked about soil and seasons, potatoes, beets, carrots and garlic. We each related stories about other gardeners in our respective areas, our associations with them, and how similar they were, despite the different environments. Some had moose and deer, we had prairie dogs and gophers.

A river flows faster in the middle: the sides run slower and are often momentarily static and clogged with debris. We can draw both sides to the middle by generating symbols of attraction, such as planting a seed, an action seemingly easy enough to do, yet it requires a certain separation from society who eats, but does not plant. Once those who have left the safe shores to perform this rite, the planting of a seed, they then become a member of a new "communitas," having shared an experience that often eludes others.

The middle stream rush of seed planting is simple, a naive thing one can do that becomes an anti-structural experience. Each season sustains in its repetition the statement of problem and solution. This is expressed first as an individual and then as a group.

The symbol of planting a seed can be powerful because it is ambiguous, and therefore full of meanings.

It is easy in this techno-complex world to garner a scoff at any belief that the individual doing something has an effect on the whole. Nevertheless, when we place a seed in the soil, we are in the middle of the stream, moving forward with other individuals whose goals are to proceed in harmony into the future.

It is an action taken rather than just spoken. It promotes a leveling of differences. It can apply in any country, to any peoples. It can be understood without language. It can bind all pasts. It can direct all futures. And as the seed grows, we can grow.

A Junco nibbling in a seed block

A SIMPLE KERNEL
Reasons to Grow

One evening, as the full moon shone brightly over the pinon trees to the east, we reflected that the days had been getting warmer, and the snow on the northeast side of the trees was retreating with the advancing sun.

Almost all of the snow in the garden had melted, and the coyote fence we built behind the garden for a windbreak, showed its effectiveness by the condition of the perennials on the west edge, which were in better condition and greening earlier than the rest.

We would enjoy shedding the few extra pounds that had accumulated during the winter months. Soon the available activities would be outside, tilling, sifting, cleaning, building, and planting.

A new season's challenges invigorated our minds as we remembered the demands of spring winds, and late frosts, obstacles presented at high altitudes, not yet completely solved. We had broadened our perspectives over the winter and would apply the knowledge gleaned from books, the internet, magazines, and other gardeners in the area.

Some friends dropped by unexpectedly on a muddy Sunday afternoon, as we were baking four small potatoes for dinner. We were able to convince them to stay and share a potato.

Along with the meal we exchanged information about how we were preparing for the summer growing season. We showed them our heating mat in the greenhouse, used for germinating seedlings, and the thermostat that controls the temperature.

They explained their outdoor "earth box" that allowed them early germination and growing before the cold had subsided. We were always interested in what actually worked for others in our area.

All too soon, they were gone but a social flavor lingered as we watched them disappear to their car parked about a quarter-mile away because of the winter road conditions.

In the garden, growth is a forward flowing fruition of value recognition; our minds can know quantity (fact), reality (idea), and meaning (relationship). But values, qualities, must be felt. It is through our associations with others (the farmer's market, friends, neighbors, and relatives) that the garden becomes an avenue for expressing core beliefs.

These links of association provide that "feeling" of value. One of the results of this "belief expression" is happiness, brought about through self-cultivation, growth, and expansion.

We heard someone once say that a truly radical thing to do was to grow your own food. This certainly appeared to be the case when one looked at the population-to-personally-grown-food ratio, (ratio is the derivational word and concept for the word reason) another "reason" to grow. This ratio probably has never been higher. Our reasons to grow values and meanings are three:

1. Energy systems (*facts*) are coherent: the proof is in the radish, and that can be acted out. Plant a radish seed and you get a radish, not a potato.

2. Reality systems (*ideas*) can be attractive: we can choose progressive systems, organic vs. non-organic, growing for just ourselves vs. sharing, staying with the "way it's always been done" vs. trying new ideas.

3. Spirit systems (*relationships*): social interaction is stabilizing, promoting a happiness that is derived from values, sought after, achieved, and then shared with others.

Values and meanings are kernels to be planted, tended, and harvested, and are the reasons that we will grow

IN-ROADS

When we were working on the new road, we took it slowly, making corrections and adjustments whenever and wherever we saw the need. In this part of the country, it is easy to make a road, in fact it is often too easy.

The weight of a vehicle will make tracks in the sand that even if impressed only once, still last until strong winds or a good hard rain softens the parallel marks. The rate of disappearing tracks is in ratio to times driven over. It didn't take many trips to make two ruts that would last for years.

Our new road went up to the hogan we were building. There was an old road part way up the hill that we had used to collect firewood. It was well imprinted from yearly trips up and down the hill gathering the winter's wood. Often it was a temptation to drive closer to where we were cutting, but then there would have been tracks everywhere.

This road ended at the foot of the hillside, at a general location that gave access to many trees, not just one. It was more work to carry the wood out, but the pleasure of unmarked land was worth it.

The next step was simply going from the end of the firewood road to the site for the hogan, driving along the bottom of the hill, which flattened out and gently sloped toward the flat valley floor. We stayed on the high side of the hill so there was a bit of a slant that followed the slope.

This slight lean was needed because the road ran along the base of a north facing rocky hill, and even though we didn't get a lot of rain, when we did it collected fast on the sandstone and gathered quickly into rivulets

Piñon Jays feeding in the winter

that turned into gullies by the time they reached the bottom of the hill.

Snow also lingered in winter, hidden in the shadows of the tall ponderosa and piñon pine. When the road did get sun and warm temperatures, the snow melted all at once and ran rapidly down the hillside.

We drove on it almost every day, each time noticing some new bump that was a rock now protruding, or a muddy spot that would need extra drainage and gravel. Flatter sections would have to be crowned for runoff. Where water had created deep gullies, we put in culverts to handle the runoff, which prevented the water from running across the road.

In some places, where we had used fresh fill to build up the road, it had become muddy and rutted. Water filled tread marks left by the backhoe we needed a week ago created mud and squished out from the tires of our truck. In time, we would correct these problems, add gravel, and make it a serviceable, daily used road.

In our rural area there is the main highway with branches of roads running off either side along the way. Some had been named by the person or persons living back in from the main road. Some were named and numbered by the state, such as BIA 125 (Bureau of Indian Affairs).

Some were dirt roads that led to cattle tanks where ranchers went in daily to break the ice and throw out some hay in the winter, calling the cattle by honking the horn as they slid along through muddy ruts.

To reach any goal there needs to be a road to get there. It may be an old one, like our road to the garden, traveled often over the years, or it may be a new one that is made in accordance with a new purpose or destination.

Some roads are in-roads, those that lead to our aspirations, following the calling of our hearts and designed by the best-laid plan of our minds. These are not one time jaunts and we may need to amend our ways each time we go until we find the right and true path that is serviceable and doesn't impact the landscape.

Someday, they will be as worn and as comfortable as the road to the garden that we know so well, and they will lead to new places where we can grow.

STRETCHING OUT

Having grown garlic for years, it was always fun to walk out to the garden and watch for the first shoots, barely peeking up through the brown winter mulch. It became doubly fun when you caught yourself making an immediate-symbol-recognition.

Our eyes knew that color and shape that carried its implied intent: to become a bulb of garlic. That garlic sprout we recognized, even at first tip, also carried an immediate symbol association: Garlic! We thought of stews with big chunks, half cloves or whole, still firm with a nip more than a bite. Gardeners, like artists, have experienced eyes.

We knew weeds from seed sprouts (most of the time). We recognized the symbol of our intent to produce a carrot, a pepper, or a radish. We recognized the shape, and the color: those cute, almost-heart-shaped radish leaves that pushed back the soil exposing themselves to the sun, or the feathery fern-like whispers of carrot leaves that came up in bunches (we always seemed to over-seed the carrots). Seeing them makes us think of carrot salad with lots of raisins. The radishes brought to mind a good friend who loved to crunch them with salt.

When a seed breaks the ground, it is acting in response to a continuation of material facts and needs that have remained intact through the ages, truths that have been proven. Gardeners are a lot like seed sprouts. We also are symbols of intent and association, and have existed, along with the plants, to provide a link to the soil and our ancestry. Often when talking with those who don't garden, they mention a parent or grandparent's garden that they remembered.

Washing off a bunch of radishes with their long white roots dangling below the sparkling red, provided the eye with a beauty that gave real satisfaction in the knowing that it was a gardener's hand that helped in their creation.

But the best part of planting, nurturing, and harvesting, was the sharing. By breaking radish with someone, we had fulfilled our intent.

Warm shirts and heavier coats were needed against the weather's intent (from the Latin, *intent*, meaning *an aim, purpose, a stretching out*). Winter had an aim and purpose, and would be stretching out until spring arrived.

A great thing about knowing other gardeners is that, when your garden is frozen out, a garden in a more protected area might still be producing. Fortunately, we have some gardening friends who, by covering their remaining crops with gunnysacks each night before the temperature dropped, had been able to keep lettuce and greens long enough to bring a wonderful salad for dinner.

Our meal helped them to fulfill an intent: that of sharing and fellowship, a culmination of effort that began months ago, stretching out unbroken until now, arriving on our plates as the snow covered the ground outside.

We eagerly awaited spring with those first green sprouts that brought a feeling of comfort in immediate-symbol-recognition, and another year of striving to express Truth, Beauty, and shared Goodness, which we would grow.

*"Poets and novelists are often moved to put
into words the subtle qualities of the landscape,
sometime purely for the beauty of it, and sometimes
as a way of alluding to certain human feelings.
Landscape design can translate such literary
landscapes into three-dimensional form in the garden.
Like the poet, the garden designer may allude to human
feelings in his portrayals of nature."*

David S. Slawson

AFTERWORD

When we first began gardening, we had a wonderful relationship with a couple of women who had a small herd of sheep on San Juan Island, Washington who could afford to give them the best of everything. Television cameras linked the birthing pens in the barn with an array of screens in their bedroom.

They carefully selected the best alfalfa from eastern Washington, which they fed to the sheep, and used for bedding inside the high tech barn. It was ferried across to the island from the mainland in semi-trailers, and it was our job each summer to assemble a crew and stack the hay barn to the rafters with the bright green bales.

Periodically we would receive a call, telling us they were going to clean the barn. On the appointed day, we would put the sideboards on our old truck and drive across the island to their farm.

Inside the barn were smooth cement floors with six to eight inches of alfalfa mixed with the sheep manure and urine than had been built up in the pens and feeders. It had been stomped on, broken into small pieces by the sheep's hooves, and kneaded into a semi-doughy consistency.

Before they bought a Bobcat with a front loader, we cleaned the barn by hand, shoveling the biggest stuff into the truck, and then using a tool like a flattened snow shovel to scrape up the rest of the compacted droppings from the floor. Once they started loading out the truck with the Bobcat it seemed like it took twice as long to unload it by hand.

We had to drive home slowly when we had a full load piled high up over the height of the cab, the weight raising the front of the truck.

Once the manure and alfalfa mixture had dried a bit, we ran it through our shredder, making a consistently textured material that we tilled directly into the garden beds, using the rest for mulch. Earthworms thrived. When we reached down under the warm mulch there were handfuls of worms working to compost it even more by adding their castings to the increasingly fertile soil.

Since sheep manure was a "cold manure" (others are rabbit, goat, or lama) it didn't have to be composted before it was added to the garden, so we didn't have to worry about it burning any of the plants, especially early in the spring when the tender seedlings sprouted.

Sheep droppings are high in nitrogen, giving the proper nutrients needed for healthy leaf growth. It was that "brown gold" that gave us incredibly vigorous plants, and made growing seem easy in the mild northwest costal climate.

We discovered the difficulties faced by people living in other areas of the country when we moved to Sedona, Arizona and began a two-acre garden project in hard red clay baked over the years into a bricklike consistency.

We used the back hoe on a 4WD Kubota to break up the clay and began the process of making soil by adding organic matter, gypsum, organic nutrients, and composted horse manure (which should be added to a garden only a couple of seasons and then avoided because of its high salt content).

We discovered there were horse stables a few miles away that had been contacted by the health department and were told to get rid of the droppings every four days so it wouldn't accumulate. They were more than happy to bring it to us in dump truck loads just to get it off their hands.

It wasn't long before we had mounds of composting horse manure mixed with produce scraps from a local health food store placed into a series of ten-by-ten foot bins built out of palate boards so that we could drive into them with the Kubota to mix and turn the compost every few weeks.

When the compost was sufficiently broken down, it was sifted, tilled into the garden beds, and used for a layer of mulch.

We put up wire fences to keep out deer and javelina, and later on built rock walls around them. Inside the fenced area we made patterned, rock wall raised beds, cemented securely to prevent water leaks.

It wasn't long before we were able to direct seed, and put in transplants, which grew well in the 3,700 foot altitude and warm air. Situated between the extreme heat of Phoenix, and the cooler Flagstaff, the gardens prospered.

Our next gardening location was near El Morro National Monument in New Mexico. We knew there were going to be challenges when shortly after our arrival a long-time resident asked us what we did, and when we replied that we were organic gardeners he responded, "That's too bad." Gardens in this high altitude 7,300-foot desert area of New Mexico were few and far between.

Our first job was to build a home. When we bought our property there was a structure started but had never been completed and came with the purchase of the land. It was a challenging project.

For the new garden area, we chose a nearby old horse corral because it had a barbed wire fence to keep out free roaming cattle. We eventually put chicken wire around the bottom of this fence to keep out rabbits and rodents, and later we added screen to keep out grasshoppers.

We kept out gophers with a three-foot trench dug around the perimeter of the garden and left it open. When the gophers dug their way toward the garden, they would see light, turn around and go back, not considering they might dig farther down and go under the open trench to reach the garden.

We had known of others who had dug gopher trenches, but they put in cinder blocks or aluminum roofing and filled the trench in with dirt, so the gophers just followed the edges down until they reached the bottom, and tunneled under them to get into the gardens.

Over the years, we had seen evidence on the far side of our trench where the gophers had poked through, seen daylight, left an open hole, and retreated. The only gophers that made it into the garden came in under the garden gate before we put bricks on the inside of the gate along the ground to stop them.

The New Mexico gardens also presented us with a fine, deep sandy soil, which over the years had leached out every possible nutrient, since rain and snowmelt easily ran down between the grains. We found that whatever organic matter and nutrients we had introduced into the soil were quickly depleted. When we stopped using the garden, the land returned to its original state.

Finding manure had been a challenge since the sheep and cattle in this area wandered all over, and there were no stables to clean.

One day we noticed a farm at Pine Hill School, and discovered a large pile of composted manure sitting alongside one of the barns, and was given away to those who needed it. We shoveled truckloads of it into our garden beds and tilled it in.

That smell of freshly tilled soil and manure, especially just after a rain, always took us back to childhood memories of our grandparent's gardens, introduced early into our young minds and hearts.

Memories formed a linking process of direction and knowledge. Whether the next link was forged in last year's garden plot, or on land that had never been worked, we had a nexus of information to use.

This garden chain secured us with direct physical links to our past, creating a continuity of effort and direction that encouraged us with the evidence that we could grow.

*"Your mind is a garden,
your thoughts are the seeds,
the harvest can be either
flowers or weeds."*

Author Unknown

The winter garden

ABOUT THE AUTHORS

The Giannangelo's began growing gardens together in 1986 on San Juan Island, off the northwest coast of Washington State not long after they were married. Starting with a small, personal vegetable garden, their enthusiasm grew into a thriving business they called, "Giannangelo Farms."

Their first garden was a sixty-foot by eighty-foot garden designed as three concentric interlocking circles, with a central fountain, and a trellised entrance covered with grape vines, and planted with culinary and medicinal herbs, and perennial flowers.

The second was a terraced garden, carved out of a hillside where they grew raspberries, globe artichokes, thirty-seven varieties of garlic, larger vegetables like broccoli, and cabbage, saffron crocus, tulips, and daffodils.

The last was a large formal, patterned, main garden with interlocking paths and trellises where they grew salad vegetables and greens, flowers, and fruit trees. Surrounding these gardens were three ponds, two aviaries, and a large lawn, all encircled by old growth forest full of Western red cedar, Douglas fir, Alder, and Hemlock.

The gardens were open to the public. They sold fresh picked vegetables, bouquets of flowers, and their own handmade products from a small porch they had turned into a storefront. Shelves were full of gardening books, their seven flavors of herbed vinegars, packages of custom mixed tea blends, and dried culinary herbs, and seeds. Dried everlasting flowers hung upside down from the ceiling in a colorful array.

They also serviced local restaurants, providing fresh herbs, salad flowers, salad greens, produce, and seasonal berries. Saturday mornings, fresh produce was taken to sell at the farmers market in the local village of Friday Harbor.

Eventually the business outgrew them and they moved to Sedona, Arizona, with an offer to build large formal gardens for a private community. In the three years they were there, they turned a hard, clay packed piece of barren land into two acres of patterned, fieldstone raised bed, formal organic vegetable, flower, and herb gardens.

Their job finished, they moved to Ramah, New Mexico, bought land, built a house, began new gardens, and established "Giannangelo Farms Southwest."

They helped establish the Ramah Farmers Market, and organized the annual Ramah Area Garden Tour. In the spring, they had a series of workshops on sustainable organic gardening, basic rockwork, labyrinths, and strawbale wall construction.

They developed an organic gardening website and reached out from their isolated area, seeking and connecting with others of like mind. A monthly gardening newsletter was sent out monthly to over one-hundred-fifty countries, available by subscription at their website, www. avant-gardening.com.

The Giannangelo's believed that the gardening experience was a method of promoting personal creativity, health, and spirituality. Their ideas and enthusiasm spread through personal and internet contact with others and created a web extending around the world, making true their watchword, "You Can Grow."

www.ingramcontent.com/pod-product-compliance
Lightning Source LLC
Chambersburg PA
CBHW081216230426
43666CB00015B/2749